The Ultimate Collection of
Computer Facts & Fun

Cindra Tison
Mary Jo Woodside

SAMS

A Division of Macmillan Computer Publishing
11711 North College, Carmel, Indiana 46032 USA

To our families, for their patience and support, with special thanks to Michael and Beau. Without them, this couldn't have happened.

Printed in the United States of America

Trademarks

This is the first four-color book to be imaged by R.R. Donnelley & Sons at 2540 dpi on the Optrotech Sprint 110 Imagesetter.

Publisher
Richard K. Swadley

Associate Publisher
Marie Butler-Knight

Managing Editor
Marjorie Jo Hopper

Acquisitions and Development Editor
Mary-Terese Cozzola Cagnina

Manuscript Editor
Barry Childs-Helton

Technical Editors
Dan Derrick and Gregg Bushyeager

Cover Design
Tim Amrhein

Cover Illustration
Ned Shaw

Designer & Production
Scott Cook, Bob LaRoche

Illustrators
Scott Cook, Barry Childs-Helton, Lyn Pusztai, Kevin Spear

Special Consultants
Jessica Butler, Rachel Derrick, T.J. Derrick,
Morgan Phillips, Beau Tison, Michael Woodside

TABLE OF CONTENTS

COMPUTER FACTS AND FUN
START HERE!

How many of these things do you think people can do with a computer?

a) Write a letter
b) Draw a picture
c) Do homework
d) Call someone at another computer
e) Play a game
f) Lift an elephant
g) Launch a rocket
h) Treat an illness
i) Feed cattle

If you said "All of the above," congratulations! You already know that computers are wonderful machines.

But do you know all the ways that computers can make your life more fun and interesting? That is what this book is about.

In this book you will find computer facts and stories. You will also find games and activities to test what you learn.

In the back of the book are answers to all the games, and a glossary to explain important terms. You can also send away for an Official Certificate when you complete all the activities!

Maybe you already know how to use computers. Maybe you are just starting to learn about them. No matter what you know so far, there are always new things to learn. So grab a pencil, turn the page, and have fun!

EARLY HISTORY *of* COMPUTERS

Before the First Computer

The idea for a computer began long ago. It began before there were televisions, before there were typewriters, even before there was paper!

Since the beginning of time, people have always invented things to make life easier.

About 50,000 years ago, cavemen learned how to build a fire to keep warm.

About 5,000 years ago, someone finally invented the wheel to move things around more easily.

And 4,000 years ago, the Chinese invented something to help them do math problems more easily. It was called an **abacus**.

The Abacus

The abacus was made of beads that moved back and forth on rods. It helped people add and subtract large numbers. Before it was invented, people could only add and subtract as many things as they could remember in their heads.

The abacus could not do most of the things a computer can do but it did one important thing that computers do. It made math problems easier for people to solve.

BUZZ WORDS

Sound Buzzwords out in the Glossary

ab•a•cus
An•a•lyt•i•cal En•gine
Bab•bage
cal•cu•la•tor
da•ta
Jac•quard
Leib•nitz
Love•lace
Pas•cal
pro•gram

Some inventions are ahead of their time.

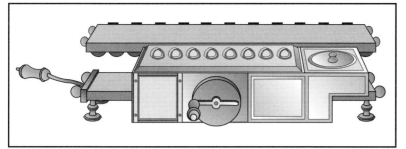

Pascal's Adding Machine

In the 1600s, a man in France invented another machine that is important in computer history. His name was Blaise **Pascal**.

Pascal worked for his father, who was a judge. Pascal had to count all the money that was paid to the court. Any time he made a mistake, he had to start counting from the beginning.

In 1641, Pascal invented an adding machine to speed up his work. His adding machine could add and subtract long columns of numbers without making a mistake. He called his machine the *Pascaline*.

The Leibnitz Calculator

A few years later, a German improved upon Pascal's invention. His name was Gottfried **Leibnitz**.

Gottfried invented a machine called the Leibnitz **Calculator**. It could do more than add and subtract. It could also multiply, divide, and find square roots of numbers. It was worked by hand.

The Jacquard Loom

Almost two hundred years later came another important machine. It was an automatic loom, invented in 1801 by Joseph-Marie **Jacquard**. This loom used information to help it make cloth.

Jacquard was a French weaver. In the 1800s, weaving was hard work. A weaver had to use his hands to string threads over and under other threads, while

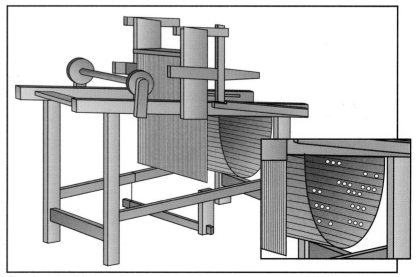

The Jacquard Loom.

his feet pumped the loom to keep it moving. He also had to choose each piece of thread as he went along, to make the cloth the right color and thickness.

Jacquard's new loom would string the threads for him while he pumped it. Joseph punched holes in cards, and hooked them together to make a pattern. The cards fed the right pieces of thread into the loom to make the cloth. Jacquard made an amazing piece of cloth. He made a set of cards that worked together to weave a picture of him!

This invention scared other weavers. It made cloth faster and more perfectly than they could. They were afraid the new loom would take away their jobs, so they burned down Jacquard's house and his new loom.

But that didn't stop Jacquard. He built the automatic loom again.

Jacquard's invention was the first machine that could use information to create something new. His loom took information from cards and used it to weave beautiful cloth.

The Analytical Engine

Charles **Babbage** lived in England during the 1800s. He wanted to build machines that could do many kinds of jobs with information. Lady Augusta Ada Byron, the Countess of **Lovelace** also lived in England. She had her own ideas about machines. She was later to invent the computer **program** (the instructions that tell a computer what to do).

In 1833, Babbage and Lovelace began working together on an invention

---

WORD SEARCH MAZE PICTURE FIND UP MATCH SORT IT ALL OUT

Here is a list of important inventions in early computer history, and a list of the people who invented them. Match up one invention with the person or people who invented it.

The machines:

Leibnitz Calculator
abacus
Analytical Engine
Jacquard Loom
Pascaline

The people:

Charles Babbage and Lady Lovelace
Gottfried Leibnitz
Blaise Pascal
People in China
Joseph-Marie Jacquard

they called an **Analytical Engine.** The word *analytical* means able to figure something out. An *engine* is a machine that works on its own, without a person moving every part.

Ahead of Their Time

Babbage and Lovelace spent years planning the Analytical Engine. They figured out how to give information to the machine, how to make it do something with the information, and how to make it give new information back.

By 1839, Babbage was working fulltime on small computing machines. Lovelace was completing her theories of how to give instructions to computers. But no one could build the Analytical Engine.

To build it, thousands of tiny parts had to be made perfectly. In the 1800s, no tools could make parts so small and exact. The Analytical Engine was never finished.

Computing machines had to wait until the 1900s.

EVEN BEFORE THE ABACUS . . .

Have you ever heard of Stonehenge? Stonehenge is a circle of big rocks on Salisbury Plain in England. The rocks were arranged that way thousands of years ago. No one today knows why. Many people have opinions about it.

The sun on the circle of rocks makes a pattern of shadows. The pattern changes slowly during the day, and it looks a different way for every season. Some people think Stonehenge was built to tell time. They call it a kind of computer, because it figures out the time of day and time of year. But nobody knows for sure if that was why it was built.

MAKE YOUR OWN ABACUS

READ ALL THE DIRECTIONS BEFORE YOU START!

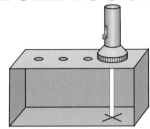

You will need:

A CARDBOARD BOX (a shoebox is fine), *AN EXTRA PIECE OF CARDBOARD* (the same size as the longest side of your box), *5 FEET OF STRING, with 28 BEADS TO STRING ON IT* (get 4 colors, 7 beads each), *STICKY TAPE, A FLASHLIGHT, A PENCIL, and SCISSORS* (ask first!)

Making the abacus:

1. Stand your box on one of its long sides, so the open side faces you.

2. Cut 4 pieces of string long enough to reach across the box, with some left over. Put them aside for later.

3. Use the tip of your scissors to punch 4 small holes (just big enough for the string to go through) in the top side of the box — like this:

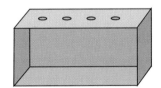

4. Shine the flashlight into the box through the first hole. Put an "X" where the light touches the bottom side. Do the same for all the holes.

5. Punch 4 small holes in the bottom side, in the middle of each "X."

6. Put your extra piece of cardboard in the box, right against the top side.

7. Push the pencil point through the first hole in the top side, to make a mark on the cardboard. Do the same thing for the last 3 holes. Take the cardboard out, and make an "X" on each of the pencil marks.

8. Punch a small hole in the cardboard, in the middle of the first "X." Punch holes in the last 3 "X" marks. Put a string through each hole.

9. Put the cardboard back in the box. Stand it up so it makes a wall between a smaller part and a bigger part of the inside, like this:

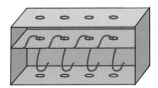

10. Tape the cardboard wall in place. Keep the ends of the strings free.

11. Sort your 28 beads into 4 color groups, with 7 beads in each group.

12. String 2 beads of the same color on the first string, in the smaller part of the box. Put this end of the string through the nearest hole, and tie a knot in the end of the string.

13. String the last 5 beads of this color on the free end of this same string, in the bigger part of the box. Put the free end of the string through the nearest hole.

14. Pull the string until it's tight, but not so tight that it bends the box. Tie a knot in the string's end outside the box, to keep it tight.

15. Use Steps 11, 12, and 13 to finish the last 3 strings in just the same way. They should look like this:

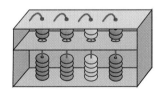

Use Your Abacus!

Lay the abacus on its back. Move all the beads against the outside walls.

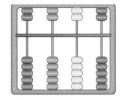

The cardboard wall divides your strings into long and short strings. The beads in each row divide into two different values: 1s on the long string, 5s on the short string.

In row 1, beads on the long string are 1s. Beads on the short string are 5s.

In row 2, beads on the long string are 10s. Beads on the short string are 50s.

In row 3, beads on the long string are 100s. Beads on the short string are 500s.

In row 4, beads on the long string are 1,000s. Beads on the short string are 5,000s.

Move the beads on a row to the inside wall to make numbers. When you are done with a calculation, move all the beads back. First, let's make some simple numbers:

21 (two "10s," one "1")
105 (one "100," no "10s," five "1s")
2,925 (Try it!)

Now let's add some numbers:
8 + 12 = ?

1. Put 8 on the abacus (one "5" bead, three "1s").

2. Now add 12. First, add the 2 (two "1" beads).

3. Now add the 10 (one "10" bead).

4. Now count up the value of your beads: one "10," one "5," and five "1s." Total: 20!

Try adding these on your own:
35 + 7 = ?
47 + 65 = ?

Before

After

THE FIRST COMPUTER

The ideas and plans of Charles Babbage and Countess Lovelace were not lost. Lovelace had taken careful notes on their work, and just fifty years after Babbage died, those notes helped someone else to build a computer. This man's name was Herman **Hollerith**. The computer he invented was not exactly the same as Babbage's computing machine, but it used many of the same ideas.

BUZZ WORDS

cen•sus

E•NI•AC

Holl•er•ith

in•te•grat•ed cir•cuit

Mark I

sil•i•con

Tab•u•lat•ing Ma•chine

tran•sis•tor

U•NI•VAC

government had a contest to find a faster way to count people.

How Did He Do It?

Herman Hollerith invented a machine called a **Tabulating Machine**. Tabulating means counting. The Tabulating Machine won the contest. The government used it in the census of 1890.

The Census

Every ten years, the government counts how many people live in the United States. This count is called a *census*. In 1880, the government took a census. But there were so many people living in the United States that it took eight years to count everyone, and to add information about where they lived and what they did for a living. Eight years was too long a time, so the

Herman's machine used cards with holes punched in them. Each hole meant one thing. One hole meant the person was married. Another one meant the person was single.

Electricity passed through the holes, and turned on motors that moved counters. The counters gave out the totals.

In 1890, it only took six weeks to perform the first simple count. A complete count was finished in only two and a half years.

Herman's new Tabulating Machine became famous. Copies of it were sold to other countries to use for their censuses. But Herman didn't stop with one invention. He started a company to build more counting machines. The company was called International Business Machines. Today it is the biggest computer company in the world. Do you recognize the name? IBM!

 ## Figure It Out

When Herman Hollerith let the government use his Tabulating Machine for the census, he didn't do it for free. He charged the government 63 cents for each 1,000 people his machine counted. For the 1890 census, the machine counted 62,622,250 people. How much money did Herman earn?

From Tabulating Machines to Computers

In the early 1900s, people all over the world invented computers that worked in ways similar to the way the Tabulating Machine worked. They did experiments to figure out how to make computers work faster, and how to make them do more than just count.

One of the first new computers was the Mark I. It was invented in 1943 at Harvard University. The **Mark I** could count faster than the Tabulating Machine, and it could do multiplication and division. After World War II, **ENIAC** did even more types of calculations.

Transistors Take Over

In those days, computers were as big as a room. Some even had almost 800,000 moving parts, and weighed 30,000 tons.

These early computers used up great amounts of power. Their parts grew so hot when they worked that air conditioners had to be built around them. With so many parts, something was always breaking.

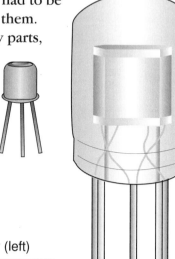

The transistor (left) replaced bulky vacuum tubes (right).

In the 1940s, the ENIAC was in a public demonstration to show that it could multiply 97,367 by 97,367 in one second. Today, there are computers which can do such calculations a million times in one second. And we don't even think twice about it!

These computers were also very hard to use. You had to be a computer scientist to even get near one.

In 1948, a group of men who worked at the Bell Laboratory took the first step toward a small, easy-to-use computer. They created the **transistor**. A transistor controls the amount of electric power that flows in and out of a wire.

Computers that used transistors could work faster than the older computers, but they were still large and hard to use.

Computers Catch On

The people building these computers were very excited about them, but not many other people were interested. These newer computers could do math faster than people, but they were still hard to use. They were still expensive to build and take care of. They still broke down all the time. People who ran businesses did not want to buy them or use them.

In 1951, a company called Sperry Univac built a computer called **UNIVAC**. Sperry fed UNIVAC input about the 1952 Presidential election. Before the results were announced, UNIVAC predicted that Dwight D. Eisenhower would win the election. UNIVAC was right!

Suddenly, people began to realize that computers could do important things for them. Businesses started to buy their own computers to solve many types of problems.

Thanks for My Walkman

When the people at Bell Laboratories invented the transistor, they didn't just use it in computers. Transistors were used to improve radios, too— now they could be smaller. Before transistors, a radio was about as big as a bookcase. (Imagine trying to carry one of those around!)

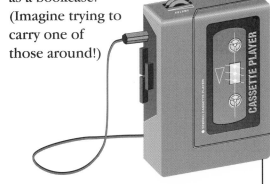

Transistors Get Left Behind

Computers were improved again in 1958. That is when the **integrated circuit** was invented. *Integrated* means combined. The integrated circuit combined—in one small place—all the parts a computer needed to run.

This meant the computer could be smaller, and have fewer parts. Information could move through it faster. Also, there were fewer parts to build, fewer parts to break, and fewer parts to fit into one machine. So computers got faster, easier to use, and much smaller.

From the Beach to the Computer

The integrated circuit was used in computers until 1968, when the computer chip was invented. The computer chip was made of silicon—which is made from sand.

The silicon chip was smaller than a dime, but it could hold all the information a computer needed to work. This allowed computers to run much faster and use less power.

Kidstuff

Today, you don't have to be a computer scientist to use a computer. Some computers are small enough to fit in your pocket. And you can simply plug a computer into a wall or use batteries to make it work. Computers can do more things with information than people dreamed of in Herman Hollerith's time. For all these reasons, computers are now very popular.

But the history of computers has not stopped yet. People continue to make improvements all the time. The idea of a computing machine is thousands of years old, but we are only beginning to see what they can do—and how much we can do with them.

WORD SEARCH
MAZE
PICTURE FIND
MATCH
UP

There are many important events in computer history. Can you remember what happened when?

Match up the events in the left-hand column with the dates in the right-hand column.

The Leibnitz Calculator was invented	1890
The silicon chip was invented	1968
Jacquard invented the automatic loom	1948
The abacus was invented	1839
The transistor was invented	about 4,000 years ago
Pascal invented the Pascaline	1958
Charles Babbage and Lady Lovelace worked on the Analytical Engine	middle 1600s
	1801
Herman Hollerith's Tabulating Machine was used in the United States Census	1641
The integrated circuit was invented	

COMPUTERS BIG AND SMALL

Today computers come in three main sizes.

The biggest computers are called **mainframes**. A mainframe can be as big as a car or even a whole room. It can handle huge jobs—like keeping track of all the people in the country, all the money in a bank, or millions of stars in a galaxy. Some mainframes have **terminals** connected — keyboards and monitors for many people to use at the same time. A mainframe can do hundreds of jobs at once. In UNIVAC's time (the 1950s), all computers were mainframes.

The in-between-size computers take up less space. You could probably fit one into a large closet. Because these computers are like small mainframes, they are called **minicomputers**.

BUZZ WORDS

com•pat•i•ble

Mac•in•tosh

main•frame

mi•cro•com•put•er

min•i•com•put•er

per•son•al

Minicomputers can handle jobs that are a little smaller than mainframe jobs. They are good for keeping track of all the people in a company, all the students in a school, or all the rainfall in a state.

The smallest computers were first made to be used by one person at a time, so they are called **personal** computers. Personal computers are small enough to sit on a desk. Some can even fit into a suitcase. Because they are so small compared to a mainframe, they are sometimes called **microcomputers** ("micro" means very small).

They are used for many different personal jobs— math, writing, playing games, or figuring out one family's income tax. This book is mostly about personal computers, because they are the ones most people use.

The two main types of personal computers are **Macintosh** and **IBM**. They look similar, and work in much the same way, but for many years they were not **compatible** (they would not work together). That is changing slowly.

How Does It Work?

A computer is different from other kinds of machines because you can do so many things with it.

Most machines only let you do one or a few things with them. You can use a pencil sharpener to sharpen a pencil. You can use a tape player to play tapes, or to record tapes. But you can use a computer to

write, draw, solve math problems, play games, and do many other activities.

You can do many things with a computer because it works in a way that is similar to the way your brain works. The computer does not work exactly like your brain but it works like your brain in many ways.

How Does Your Brain Work?

To understand how a computer works, think about how your brain works. You do more things and have more thoughts every day than you can count. But for all of your different thoughts and activities, your brain follows the same few steps:

1 Your brain takes in information.

2 Your brain remembers information.

3 You can think about any information in your brain.

4 When you change your mind, the information in your brain changes.

5 You give out information whenever you talk, write, or do an action.

Five Simple Steps

A computer works by following these five steps, too. There are special computer words for these steps.

1 Step 1. It takes information you put in. The information that the computer takes in is called **input**.

2 Step 2. It remembers information so you can use it later. When the computer remembers information, it **stores** the information.

3 Step 3. It shows you information so you decide what to do with it. When the computer shows you information, it **displays** the information.

4 It changes the information when you want it to. When the computer changes information, it **edits** the information

5 It gives out information so you can share it with others. The information that the computer gives out is called **output**.

Similar but Different

Y our brain and a computer work in a similar way. But they are very different from each other. Here are a few of the differences:

A computer can do the same job over and over again, without getting tired or bored, and without making a mistake.

A computer can work more quickly than people. It's amazing just how fast it can work. People who are VERY good at adding numbers can add them up in

a few seconds. A computer can add up the same numbers—and still have the time to add up THOUSANDS more—in just ONE second!

A computer can remember information for years, without forgetting a single word or number.

Are Computers Smarter Than People?

Of course not! Computers can only do these wonderful things because of us. We give them information. We give them commands. Without information and commands, a computer cannot think.

But people can think for themselves. We can get information and commands from other people, but we can also think up our own. This difference is more important than all the other differences between people and computers. We can choose to use a computer or not.

Computers are special machines because we can use them in so many different ways—but a computer is still just a machine. You can do more things with a computer than you can with a toaster. But if no one is using the computer or the toaster, neither machine can do anything.

Word Search

Each of the words in this list is hidden in this jumble of letters. How many of the words can you find?

INPUT	EDIT	PERSONAL
STORE	OUTPUT	COMPUTER
DISPLAY	IBM	TRANSISTOR
	SILICON	

```
T A L A N O S R E P
B R E T U P M O C A
T T D E R O N T F R
L U U I I S O S R P
I P M T S T C I S M
N T T B P P I S F O
P U B T I T L N O C
U O E D I T I A A I
T O T O L A S R Y N
I R N I E R O T S O
```

COMPUTER

A computer may look like just one machine, but it is made of many different machines. There is the computer itself, plus all the parts used with it. Each part by itself is called a **peripheral**. The computer and peripherals work together, but they each do different jobs. When they work together they are called a **system**. The parts of a system are **components**.

1 You use a keyboard to type letters and numbers into the computer, and to move to different parts of the screen.

2 You use a mouse to point to different parts of the screen. It works faster than the keyboard for this. You can also draw with it!

3 The **central processing unit** (CPU) is the computer chip or chips that put information through a

process. It stores input, carries out commands, and creates output. The CPU also remembers information.

4 The **circuit board** is connected to everything else in the computer. Electricity travels along the circuit board from the power supply to the **silicon chips.** The silicon chips process and store information.

5 The **monitor** shows you output on a screen.

6 The **modem** is a sort of telephone for the computer. The modem is attached to a phone line, and carries both input and output.

7 The **printer** prints output onto paper.

8 The **hard disk** stores all the information you save on your computer. The information you save stays on the hard disk even after you turn off the computer. You can use the information again, whenever you want.

9 These are **floppy disks,** also known as **diskettes**. They can be put in and taken out of the computer. Floppy disks do not hold nearly as much information as the hard disk, but you can use as many of them as you want.

10 The **disk drive** holds floppy disks. When a floppy disk is in the disk drive, the disk drive can take input off the disk, or put output on it.

QWERTY? WHAT'S THAT?

Qwerty is the name for the way the alphabet appears on a keyboard. The letters of the alphabet are placed in the same order on every computer keyboard. This makes it easy to remember where they are when you type. To see where the name "qwerty" comes from, look at the alphabet keys in the upper left-hand corner of the keyboard. What do they spell?

BUZZ **W O R D S**

cen•tral proc•ess•ing
   u•nit
disk drive
disk•ette
key•board
mo•dem
mon•i•tor
mouse
pe•riph•er•al
sil•i•con chip
sys•tem

FIND THE COMPUTER PARTS

Five computer parts are hidden in this picture. How many of them can you find?

DOWN MEMORY LANE

Different Kinds of Memory

You have learned that memory stores all instructions and information for the computer. But did you know that there are three different kinds of memory?

If you think about all the different kinds of things the computer has to remember, it makes sense.

1. It has to remember how to follow each step in the processing path.

2. It has to remember instructions and information you put into it.

3. It has to remember instructions and information you save in it.

ROM, RAM and Storage

The three kinds of memory a computer has are called **Random-Access Memory**, **Read-Only Memory**, and **Storage**.

 Read-Only Memory remembers what order the computer should work in. The control unit in the CPU keeps information moving from step to step. It uses Read-Only Memory to keep the steps in the right order.

Without Read-Only Memory, the computer would not know that it should take information in before it displays it on the screen. It would not know how to send output to the printer. Things would be a mess.

But you can depend on Read-Only Memory. It never forgets the right order things should work in. People who know about Read-Only Memory like to call it *ROM* for short.

 *Random-Access Memory* remembers instructions and

BUZZ WORDS

file
flopp•y disk
hard disk
mag•net•ic disk
Ran•dom-Ac•cess
  Mem•o•ry
Read-On•ly Mem•o•ry
Stor•age

information you put into the computer. While the computer is on it uses information and instructions from Random-Access Memory to obey your commands. When you turn off the computer, Random-Access Memory forgets everything. When you turn the computer on again, it will not remember the information and instructions you gave it last time. Random-Access Memory is called *RAM* for short.

Storage hold's information, and instructions you give the computer to save. **Magnetic Disks** (which work much like cassette tapes) are one form of storage. There are two types: **hard disks** and **floppy disks**. The hard disk inside the computer stores a lot of information and instructions. It is a great place to store *programs,*

WORD SEARCH

NUMBER 2

Find these hidden words:

MODEM
COMPUTER
COMPONENT
CPU
ABACUS
TERMINAL
PROCESSOR
PATH
MAGNETIC
ENIAC
FLOPPY
KEYBOARD

```
P L A A R G H E W G
R F F M H R N C X D
O L Q P T I O I O R
C O N W A M U T R A
E P U C P U L E F O
S P A U R F I N U B
S Y T L N O O G G Y
O E S U C A B A F E
R A B M E D O M I K
O F L A N I M R E T
T N E N O P M O C L
```

which are sets of instructions for different activities. It is a good place to store information you work with often.

Floppy disks store information too. They are useful because you can use them to exchange information with other people and in other computers. When you store something on a floppy disk instead of on a hard disk, you save storage space in the hard disk. This is important if you have lots of programs and information you want to store there.

Files of Information

When you tell the computer to save some information you are working on, the

Chips

Read-Only Memory and Random-Access Memory come in *chips*. The chips are attached to the circuit board of the computer.

information is put into its own **file**. The file of information is saved on a disk. *All* information that is saved, is saved in a file.

A file is kind of like a folder. Let's say you are writing on a report for school. Halfway through writing, you decide to stop for a while. To keep the report and all your notes safe, you put them all in a folder. Then you put the folder in a drawer.

There is an important difference between paper files and computer files. When you work on paper, you do not have to put your report and notes into a folder. You do not have to put the folder in a drawer.

But with the computer, you do have to save your information in a file, and you have to put the file on a disk.

After all, you could always hunt through the house for your paper report. But how would you hunt through a computer?

Only two of these disks can go into disk drives!

WRAPPING IT ALL UP:
THE PROCESSING PATH

When you give information and instructions to your computer, they go in through an input device. Then your input follows a **path** through the computer.

This is the path your input follows:

From your input device, the input travels into the computer and goes to the CPU inside it.

The processor is made of silicon chips. It has three main parts: the **Control Unit**, **Memory,** and the **Arithmetic Logic Unit**.

The Control Unit moves your information from one step to the next. First it stores your input in Random-Access.

Next, the Control Unit takes instructions from storage Memory, and sends them to the Arithmetic Logic Unit.

The Arithmetic Logic Unit follows the instructions and creates some new information.

The Arithmetic Logic Unit sends the new information back to Memory.

Memory stores the new information.

The Control Unit turns the new information into output.

The output comes to you through a peripheral like a monitor or printer.

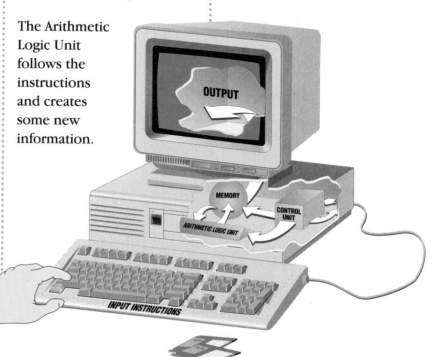

PERSONAL COMPUTERS AND
WORLD EVENTS

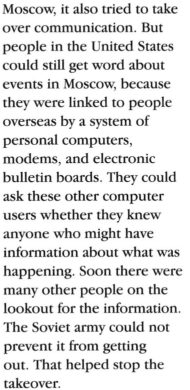

E arly mainframes cost millions of dollars to build — only governments and businesses could afford them. Governments used computers for planning how to respond to world events. By 1970, for example, the Pentagon was using IBM mainframes to figure out how to fight wars in space. By the 1990s, world events could reach right into the home through a personal computer!

Passing the Word

In August 1991, when the Soviet army took over Moscow, it also tried to take over communication. But people in the United States could still get word about events in Moscow, because they were linked to people overseas by a system of personal computers, modems, and electronic bulletin boards. They could ask these other computer users whether they knew anyone who might have information about what was happening. Soon there were many other people on the lookout for the information. The Soviet army could not prevent it from getting out. That helped stop the takeover.

Causing a Stir

At the same time, a publisher of computer games was almost ready to publish a new game by a Soviet immigrant living in the United States. His name was Vladimir Baculyn, and his game was called "Crisis in the Kremlin." It was about the Soviet army taking over Moscow! Now Baculyn's publisher was rushing to put the game on the market. In a TV interview, Baculyn said he'd thought up the game long before the takeover. He had made his game realistic, so it could show the American public how difficult Russia's problems were. But games are also fun — and when they are about real events, they can make fun of someone else's suffering, without meaning to. What do you think?

Imagine you are the president of a French company that makes computer games. One day, one of your workers rushes into your office with a newspaper. The front page shows a riot in Washington, D.C., with National Guard tanks in the streets, and the headline: "Revolution in America?" Your worker tells you she knows about a computer game invented by an American who lives in Paris. The game is called "Crisis in the Capitol," about the National Guard taking over Washington, D.C. Your company can put it on the market right away. What do you do?

THINK ABOUT IT

THE "DISAPPEARING MEMORY" EXPERIMENT!

"These letters disappear right out of my head! Can YOU remember them for me?"

You'll need: *A PENCIL, 4 SHEETS OF PAPER, A SHEET OF CARDBOARD, A CLOCK OR WATCH, AND A FRIEND TO BE YOUR TEST SUBJECT.*

People have a short-term memory that works a lot like RAM. This experiment will show you how short-term memory works. All you have to do is follow the directions. All your friend has to do is to remember the letters on the Professor's two blackboards, and write them down. But that may be harder than it looks!

The Snap Test:

1. Put your sheet of cardboard over the Professor's blackboards, so they can't be seen, and give your friend a blank sheet of paper and the pencil.

2. Tell your friend, "I'm not going to speak during this test. I'll show you some letters for a few seconds, then I'll cover them. Wait until I snap my fingers. Then write down the letters you saw. Write as many as you can remember. I'll snap again when it's time to stop."

3. Move the cardboard so your friend can see the letters on Blackboard 1. In five seconds, cover the letters again. (Don't speak yet.)

4. Wait 10 seconds, then snap your fingers. (Don't speak now!) It's time for your friend to start writing.

5. Wait for 30 seconds while your friend is writing, and snap your fingers when the 30 seconds are up.

6. When your friend puts down the pencil, it's time to do the Sonic Word Test.

The Sonic Word Test:

1. Ask your friend to turn over the first sheet of paper, and take out a new sheet of blank paper to write on.

2. Tell your friend, "This test will be the same as the last one. But this time, instead of making a noise, I'll *say* when to begin writing and when to stop."

3. Move the cardboard and show your friend the letters on Blackboard 2. Wait five seconds, then cover the letters again. (Don't speak yet.)

4. Wait 10 seconds. (Just like last time—Ssshh!) When 10 seconds are up, say to your friend, "Go ahead and write down the letters you remember."

5. Wait for 30 seconds while your friend is writing. (Don't talk yet!) When 30 seconds are up, say, "Time's up now."

6. When your friend puts down the pencil, you're ready to compare your results.

Compare Your Results:

1. Have your friend turn over the sheet of paper that has the letters from Blackboard 1 on it (Snap Test answer). How many letters are in the Snap Test answer?

2. Now have your friend turn over the paper that has the letters from Blackboard 2 on it (Sonic Word Test answer). How many letters are in the Sonic Word Test answer?

3. Which answer has more letters? Write down how many letters were in each of your friend's answers.

Check Your Results:

1. Now let your friend test you!

2. How did you do? Which test let you remember more letters?

"DISAPPEARING MEMORY" EXPERIMENT ANSWER: The Snap Test usually shows *more* letters remembered. The Sonic Word Test usually shows *fewer* letters remembered. Here's why. Your brain has *short-term memory* and *long-term memory*, just like your computer. (Short-term memory remembers things that happened recently—but nothing else. Long-term memory remembers things that happened a long time ago.) When you showed your friend the blackboards, your friend's short-term memory "recorded" the letters. The sound of snapping your fingers didn't bother this "recording." But when you TOLD your friend to stop writing, instead of snapping your fingers, your words "erased" some of the letters stored in your friend's short-term memory. Then there weren't as many letters left in there to write down!

PRINTING

Printers are a popular output device. They turn electronic signals from the CPU into a form we can share with others. The output you get from a printer is called a *printout*.

The two main types of printers are laser printers and dot-matrix printers.

The Laser Printer

Laser printers make the highest quality printouts. They work faster than any other printer. The only problem is, they are very expensive.

How It Works

A laser printer works much like a copy machine. It uses information from the computer instead of a picture we feed in.

The computer uses a laser to draw a magnetic picture on a metal drum inside the printer. As the drum turns around, it

passes through black powder called toner. The toner sticks to the magnetized picture on the drum. Next the drum rolls over paper, and the toner is rolled on the paper. Finally the paper is heated up and the toner melts onto it like ink.

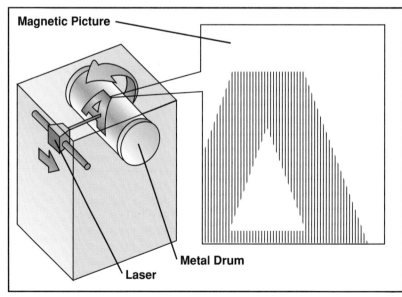

Magnetic Picture

Metal Drum

Laser

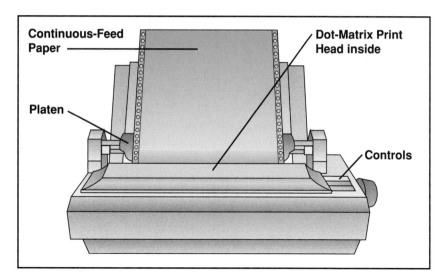

Continuous-Feed Paper

Dot-Matrix Print Head inside

Platen

Controls

When the pins receive the signals from the computer, they push against the paper quickly. The pins leave a trail of dots as they move across the paper. The dots, which are set close together, form the letters and pictures.

When the pins push against the ribbon and paper, they are acting as a *matrix*. A matrix is something that forms something else inside of it. In this case, the letter A is formed out of the dots (as you can see in the picture). This is how the printer got the name dot matrix.

Dot-Matrix Printers

The **Dot-Matrix Printer** is the most popular type of printer. It is easy to use and not too expensive. On most dot-matrix printers, the paper goes in the back, gets pulled down under a roller called the **platen**, and ends up in the front. It's a lot like putting paper in a typewriter. This paper can either be a single sheet, as with a typewriter, or **continuous-feed paper**. Continuous-feed paper is like one long sheet that feeds through the printer. It comes apart into seperate sheets when the printing is done.

How It Works

A dot-matrix printer has a ribbon like a typewriter. It makes a printout by using small pins inside the print head. The computer sends the printer signals that tell which pins should push against the ribbon and touch the paper with ink.

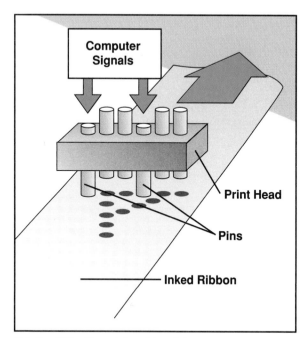

Computer Signals

Print Head

Pins

Inked Ribbon

Printing "A" with a dot-matrix printer.

JUMP SHOT on the DOT

A good example of a dot matrix is the electronic scoreboard at basketball games. Notice that each score shows up as a pattern of dots. The windows that show the scores are set up like dot-matrix print heads, but instead of pins, they have lights. The lights are arranged in eight columns. In the scoreboard shown it takes four columns to show the number two.

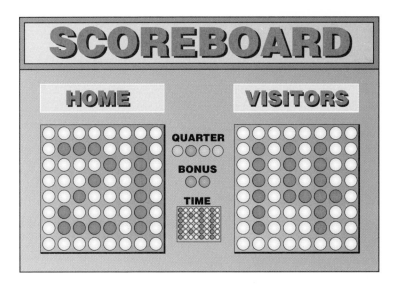

Mission Possible

There is a message hidden in the empty dots. Your mission is to find out what it is. You'll have to "print" like a dot-matrix printer to figure out the message. The numbered instructions will tell you which dots to fill. These instructions are like the instructions the CPU gives to the printer.

For a real challenge, time yourself. Write down your time when you have finished. You will need it to figure out your speed.

Example: Column 1 - fill A (The "A" dot in column 1 is filled in.)

READY TO START? GO!

Column 2	Fill B
Column 3	Fill C
Column 4	Fill D,E,F,G,H,I
Column 5	Fill C
Column 6	Fill B
Column 7	Fill A
Column 8	Fill C,D,E,F,G
Column 9	Fill B,H
Column 10	Fill A,I
Column 11	Fill A,I
Column 12	Fill B,H
Column 13	Fill C,D,E,F,G
Column 14	Leave Blank
Column 15	Fill A,B,C,D,E,F,G
Column 16	Fill H

Column 17	Fill I
Column 18	Fill I
Column 19	Fill H
Column 20	Fill A,B,C,D,E,F,G
Column 21	Leave Blank
Column 22	Fill all the dots
Column 23	Fill A,I
Column 24	Fill A,I
Column 25	Fill B,H
Column 26	Fill C,D,E,F,G
Column 27	Leave Blank
Column 28	Fill all the dots
Column 29	Leave Blank
Column 30	Fill all the dots
Column 31	Fill A,I
Column 32	Fill A,I

Column 33	Fill B,H
Column 34	Fill C,D,E,F,G,
Column 35	Leave Blank
Column 36	Leave Blank
Column 37	Leave Blank
Column 38	Fill all the dots
Column 39	Leave Blank
Column 40	Fill A
Column 41	Fill A
Column 42	Fill all the dots
Column 43	Fill A
Column 44	Fill A
Column 45	Leave Blank
Column 46	Leave Blank
Column 47	Fill A,B,C,D,E,F,G,I

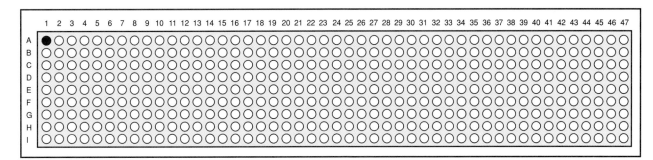

How did you do?

Write down your time in the purple box below

Now divide it by 9.

Write the result in the blank space below.

I "printed" _____ characters per minute.

Quick Click

A dot-matrix printer is so fast we count its speed in characters per second. The slowest dot-matrix prints about 80 characters in a second. Printing this message would take a slow printer less than a second.

FONT fun

BUZZ WORDS

font

type•face

A **font** is a name for one complete set of letters, numbers, and symbols that are all the same style. A font is also called a **typeface**.

The word typeface comes from the days when all print was typed with metal molds. The style of a letter was its face.

You can use different fonts to express the mood you are in.

Feeling JAZZY? This is Bodini Poster font.

Or maybe you want to be fancy...Use this Zapf Chancery font.

Or maybe just a little bit offbeat? Try this Keyboard font.

Sometimes you can *get even kookier* by changing fonts in the middle of a sentence **and then back again.**

Fonts make writing more fun!

BREAK THE CODE

How are your powers of detection? Can you figure out what this message is saying? The message was typed using a plain old everyday keyboard. But the font used to type it was no ordinary font. This font makes one symbol for each letter of the alphabet. For example, when you type "A" on your keyboard the CPU tells the printer to print a " ♩ " in its place. When you type a "B," the CPU tells the printer to print an " 🍓 ."

Can you break the code? Here are some clues to help you:

🏢 = E

〰 = I

✉ = S

🏠 = R

🍇 = C

👣 = N

🛹 = F

🚃 = G

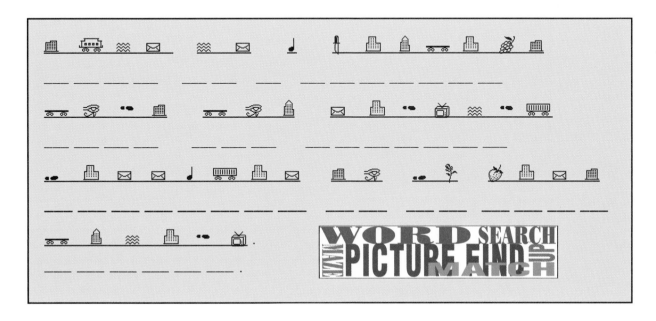

MODEMS

How would you like to talk, play games, and learn new things from people you've never met, all while sitting at your computer? How about doing research for a school report without leaving the house? Or leaving a message on your best friend's computer without going into his house? You can do all this and more using a computer modem.

A modem lets you share information, pictures, and even computer programs with computers all over the world.

How Does It Work?

A modem is a telephone for your computer. It is attached to your computer and also hooked up to a telephone line. To connect with another computer, your modem has to dial the telephone number of the other modem. Once the connection is made, you communicate by typing messages.

When you type a message into the computer,

the modem turns the input into tiny sound signals. The sound signals go out over the telephone wires as easily as your voice does.

If you could hear what was going through the wire, it wouldn't sound much like a human voice. Modem signals sound more like radio static.

Your message appears on the other computer's screen. When they reply, their message appears on your screen.

Your push-button phone can be an input device!

ELECTRONIC BULLETIN BOARDS

Bulletin boards are great places for sharing information. You probably see school bulletin boards covered with lunch menus, homework assignments, lost and found items, birthday notices, and special awards.

There are services that can bring information like this—and more—right to your computer. This type of service is called an **online service**. CompuServe, PC-Link, and PRODIGY are online services. One of the features they offer is an **electronic bulletin board**. It's also known as a **Bulletin Board Service** (BBS for short).

A BBS works much like the real bulletin boards you've seen—many people put their information in the same place, so it can be shared. An electronic bulletin board holds a huge amount of information, however. All the computers that are connected to it can use it.

Some electronic bulletin boards provide games, activities, discussions and electronic mail.

Others give information about just one subject, like sports, cooking, or science. One BBS, for example, is devoted entirely to earthquakes. It's called the Earthquake Information Center and this BBS contains data on earthquakes all over the world.

Ask a parent to help you choose a bulletin board—and always get permission before you join any BBS. You will want to consider the cost of using the BBS, any long-distance costs for the modem's phone line, and the kinds of services the BBS provides. CompuServe, PC-Link and PRODIGY each has a BBS just for kids. One of them may be a good place to start.

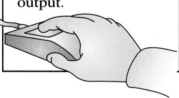

A modem is a very unusual peripheral. It handles both input *and* output.

A-MAZE-ING POWERS!

Help! A computer in the United States wants to send information by modem to a computer in Australia. There is only one way to connect them. Can you find it?

COMPUTER PROGRAMMING

We tell computers what to do by giving them commands. For example, you might be using a computer to write a letter. If you want to check the spelling of the letter, you might use your mouse to click on a command that says "Check Spelling." How does the computer know what you are asking for? That is what computer programming is all about.

Computers don't understand English, but there are people who understand computer language. These people are called computer programmers. Programmers write instructions that teach computers how to understand and obey commands from people. Each set of instructions is a computer program.

The program has to hold all the different steps you might want to follow. There are steps for writing and printing a letter. There are other steps for playing a video game. There are different steps for doing math homework. The program has to tell the computer which steps to follow.

Each program also has instructions for you. When you buy a program, the instructions are included. They tell you how to use the program, and what commands to give it.

If there were no computer programs, you would have to write every instruction for the computer yourself. You would have to write the instructions in computer language—and you would have to write the instructions out VERY carefully. If you made even one mistake, or forgot something, the program would not work.

WRITING A
COMPUTER PROGRAM

Learning a computer language is not exactly like learning a spoken language such as English or Spanish. Once you learn enough Spanish words, and how to make sentences out of them, you can speak Spanish. But with a computer language, you have to learn how to put your sentences together *perfectly*.

Before you start giving commands to the computer, you have to think through every step of what you want it to do. If you miss any steps, the program will not work.

Let's say you have a robot. You want this robot to throw out the garbage for you.

Here is one possible program you could write for the robot:

1. Carry this garbage to the garbage can.

2. The garbage cans are beside the garage.

3. Put the garbage in a garbage can.

Will that work? No way! How will the robot get out of the house? What if there is something in between the house and the garbage cans? And how about the cans? Where exactly ARE the cans? Beside the garage? Which side of the garage? How many sides does the garage have? What should the robot do when it is finished?

Let's try again:

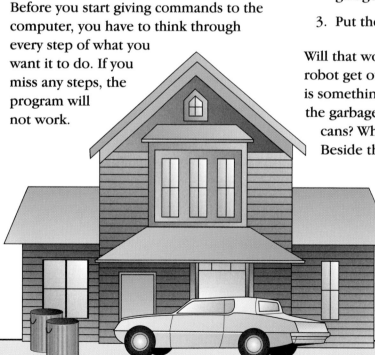

1. Take the garbage bag to the back door.

2. Open the back door.

3. Go down three stair steps.

4. Walk straight, fifteen steps.

5. Turn right.

6. Walk straight, five steps.

7. Turn right.

8. Reach down.

9. Take off the garbage can's lid.

10. Put the garbage bag inside the garbage can.

11. Turn left.

12. Walk straight, five steps.

13. Turn left.

14. Walk straight, fifteen steps.

15. Go up three stair steps.

16. Open the back door.

17. Enter the house.

18. Close the door.

Did we miss anything?

WORD SEARCH
MAZE PICTURE FIND UP
MATCH

DO YOU SPEAK BINARY?

The information we feed into the computer turns into electronic pulses. The pulses are its language.

We can use thousands of words to communicate. But an electronic pulse doesn't have many choices. It is either on or off. That's it. The computer has to use those two choices, on or off, to handle all the information we give to it. The language built around those two choices is called **binary** code.

Let's look at how those two simple choices let us communicate with a computer.

Inside the CPU, electronic pulses move through the circuit board to the computer chips. Each computer chip has millions of tiny switches, arranged in sets. Each of these sets has seven switches to use for communicating. When an electronic pulse reaches a set, it turns the switches on and off, in an exact order.

ASC•II
bi•na•ry

We use a "1" to mean the switch is on, and a "0" to mean the switch is off. Each letter of our alphabet has its own pattern of "ons" and "offs". Look at these examples.

G = 1000111. This means the first switch is ON, the next three are OFF, and the last three switches are ON.

O = 1001111. This means the first switch is ON, the next two are OFF, and the last four are ON.

When you type "GO" on your keyboard, here is what the computer turns it into:

10001111000111

Now the computer knows which switches to turn on, and which to turn off. Now it can obey your command.

But that's a lot of numbers to read, process, and turn back into English. It looks like this would take a long time, doesn't it?

It would—if a person had to do it. Computers are faster because they use electricity to move information. Millions of electronic pulses pass through a computer chip every second. The computer can translate your input, string the combinations together, process them, and turn them back into English before you can blink.

Binary code by itself is impossible for programmers to use, but maybe you have a knack for it. Are you ready for a challenge?

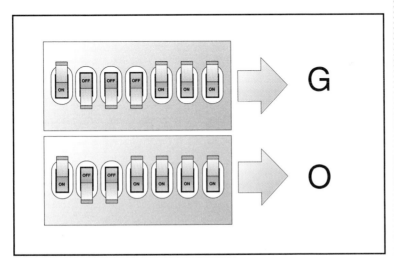

To a computer, 1 means "on" and 0 means "off."

BREAK THE CODE

L isted below is a sample of a real binary code: the American Standard Code for Information Interchange (**ASCII**, pronounced "ASK-ee," for short). Under each letter is a column of 1's and 0's. That column is what the computer reads (remember, a computer reads faster than a human being can).

```
A B C D E F G H I J K L M N O P Q R S T U V W X Y Z

1 1 1 1 1 1 1 1 1 1 1 1 1 1 1 1 1 1 1 1 1 1 1 1 1 1
0 0 0 0 0 0 0 0 0 0 0 0 0 0 0 0 0 0 0 0 0 0 0 0 0 0
0 0 0 0 0 0 0 0 0 0 0 0 0 1 1 1 1 1 1 1 1 1 1 1 1 1
0 0 0 1 0 1 0 1 1 1 1 1 1 1 0 0 0 0 0 0 0 0 1 1 1
0 0 0 1 1 1 1 0 0 0 1 1 1 1 0 0 0 0 1 1 1 1 0 0 0
0 1 1 0 0 1 1 0 0 1 1 0 0 1 1 0 0 1 1 0 0 1 1 0 0 1
1 0 1 0 1 0 1 0 1 0 1 0 1 0 1 0 1 0 1 0 1 0 1 0 1 0
```

Now test your skill. Below is a message written in ASCII binary code. Can you solve it?

```
1 1 1 1 1 1 1 1 1 1 1 1 1 1 1
0 0 0 0 0 0 0 0 0 0 0 0 0 0
0 0 0 0 1 0 1 1 0 0 1 0 0 0 1
0 1 1 0 0 0 0 1 0 0 1 1 1 0
0 1 1 1 0 0 1 1 1 0 1 0 1 1 0
1 1 1 1 1 0 0 0 0 0 0 0 1 1 1
1 1 0 1 0 1 0 1 0 1 0 1 1 0 1
```

_____

(Write your answer here)

COMPUTER LANGUAGES

BUZZ **WORDS**

high-lev•el lan•guage

op•er•at•ing sys•tem

se•quence

In the 1950s programmers got tired of struggling with binary code. They began inventing languages that the computer could translate into binary code for itself. After the computer translates the language, it can obey it.

We think of these languages as a "step up" from writing in binary code. That is why they are called **high-level languages**.

Programmers use different high-level languages to write different types of programs.

Here are some of the most popular high-level languages. Some of them were named after famous people.

FORTRAN: This language is used to write scientific programs, such as the ones for predicting the weather.

COBOL: This language is used to write many business programs, such as the ones for sending out bills and calculating paychecks.

PASCAL: This language is often used to teach people how to program. (Named after Blaise Pascal!)

BASIC: (Beginners All-Purpose Symbolic Instructional Code) This is

0110010

one of the easiest computer languages to learn. It uses many English words. People who are just beginning to program often choose to learn BASIC first.

ADA: This language was developed for the U.S. Department of Defense. It is used to write programs for secret defense and aerospace projects. (Named after Countess Lovelace!)

C: This language is used to write common programs that do many different tasks. Some of the programs it writes are word processors, graphics, and **operating systems**. Operating systems are programs that tell the computer how to run other programs.

Today, programs are written in these and many other computer languages. But to use a program, you do not have to know anything about the language it is written in. You just have to know what you want to use it for.

That can be harder than it sounds. There are more computer programs in the world than anyone could use in a lifetime. How do you decide which ones are right for you?

You can start by asking the right questions. Here are four:

1. What am I interested in?

2. What do I need to do about my interests?

3. How could a computer help me?

4. Is there any software that will do what I want my computer to do?

DON'T ASCII ME!!

We can't speak to the computer in its "native language," because that "language" is electricity! Programming languages were invented to "translate" our commands into electricity. When we give the computer a command, the programming language changes the words and numbers we use into a **sequence** of electric pulses (that means they come one after another). These pulses set the parts of the computer in motion. That is how it obeys our commands. We know the computer has understood us when it gives us output in our own language. It can give us this output because the programming language has changed the computer's electric pulses back into words and numbers. Binary code is just the way we keep track of what's going on inside the computer. It's nearly impossible for people to use binary code to talk to each other. (Try it!) But almost any computer can understand ASCII binary code.

SOFTWARE

A computer is made of **hardware**—the keyboard, monitor, CPU, cable, and all the other solid parts. These many kinds of parts are what make a computer able to work. "Hardware" is a good word to use when you are talking about all of the parts at once.

Programs are not hardware. They are sets of instructions that tell the computer what to do. This makes them just as important as hardware. **Software** is a good word to use when you are talking about programs of all kinds.

Categories and Types

There are many *categories* of software, and many different *types*

within each category. To understand the difference between categories and types, think about fruit.

The categories of fruit are apples, oranges, strawberries, bananas, and so on. Within each category, there are many types. In the apple category, for instance, there are many types to choose from. You might want a Granny Smith apple, a Red Delicious, a Macintosh apple, or some other type of apple.

There are many categories of software, like games, word processors, graphics, and so on. Within each category, there are many types. In the "games" category of software, you

could choose a mystery game, strategy game, or another type of game.

How Does it Work?

A program is recorded on floppy disks, which only a computer can read. You have to **install** the disks in your computer. Installing means putting each floppy disk into the disk drive so information can be loaded into your computer

After you install a piece of software, the information

is still on the floppy disk. Installing just copies the information. It doesn't take anything away from the floppy disk. The disk keeps the information in case your computer breaks, or you get a new computer. Then you have to install the software again.

Software Publishers

If a programmer writes a program that many people may want to buy, there are other people who will get the new program ready to sell. They work in companies which make copies of the software to sell. These companies are software **publishers**.

First, the publisher looks for any mistakes or places that the program could be better. Once these mistakes are fixed, thousands of copies of the program are made.

Directions for using the software are written, and packages to hold the program are made. Finally, copies of the program are sold to stores and through the mail.

True Crime

Let's say your mom buys you a great new program. You install it on your computer and ask your friend over to see it. Your friend loves the program. She wants a copy for her computer. But her mom will not let her buy one.

Grammar Check

The word "software" is used just the way hardware is. It is always used in the plural. You do not buy a hardware, and you do not buy a software. You might buy a piece of hardware, like a printer, and you might buy a piece of software, like a game.

Your friend asks you to let her "borrow" the program. You know she will give the disks right back after she installs them. You want your friend to enjoy the program too. Do you let her install the program?

If you do, you are committing a crime. Installing software that is not yours is stealing. If you let someone else install your software on their computer, you are helping that person to steal.

Most software is protected by copyright laws. **Copyright** means that the software must not be copied without getting permission first from the people who made the software. Copyright laws also protect books, records, and movies.

But software is so easy to install that many people forget about the copyright.

People who would never think of stealing a car might not think it's wrong to install someone else's software on their own computer. After all, who does it hurt?

It hurts the people who write, publish, and sell software to make a living. Programmers work hard to write good programs. Software companies work hard to make and distribute the software. Stores work hard to sell it. Each of these people gets paid a little bit for every copy of the program that is sold. If you install a program without paying for it, you are taking away some of the money each of these people earned—whether you mean to or not.

Installing someone else's software hurts us, too. Many software publishers have to raise the price of software to make up for all the software that is installed illegally.

Free To The Public!

Some software is free to be used by anyone. This software is called **public domain** software. That means anyone can use or copy it. Public domain software is not protected by copyright laws. It is the only kind of software that you can legally copy for other people—except, of course, any programs you write yourself!

You can help stop software crime. You can promise not to install any program that is not yours, and not to lend your copies out. You can explain to other people why it is wrong to install software that is not theirs.

Can you think of other ways to help?

PROCESS THEM!

Word processors are very popular computer programs. Using a word processor is kind of like having your own teacher inside the computer who helps you with your work as you go along. The only difference is, you don't have to keep rewriting your work! Instead, you type in the changes you want, and print out a new copy that looks exactly the way you want it to.

Important Terms

Before you can understand word processing, you have to know some important terms:

Character: a letter, number, punctuation mark, or symbol.

Cursor: a dot of light on the computer screen that tells you where the next character will go.

Document: anything you write on your word processor. It can be a letter or a report or a poem, a recipe, or any other file.

File: any document that you save in your word processor.

BUZZ

char•ac•ter
cur•sor
doc•u•ment
ed•it•ing
save
the•sau•rus
word pro•cess•or

How It Works

First, you type into the keyboard just as if you were using a typewriter.

You use special function keys to erase words, move sentences around, and add new sentences. These steps are called **editing**.

Some word processing programs check for spelling mistakes, and have a **thesaurus**. A thesaurus helps you think of other words to use. Some can even correct the grammar you have used.

When you are ready, you can press a button to print your work and a copy rolls out of the printer.

After you read it, you decide that the first and the second paragraph should be moved around. Do you make this change? Well, if you had to write out this work again by hand, you'd probably never do it—you'd just leave it the way it was. But with a word processor you can go back into the work, make your changes, and print it out again.

Like other programs you can **save** your word processing work. If you start something and don't want to finish it right away, you can just save it in a file, and come back to it another day.

THE GREAT KEYBOARD SPECIAL KEY HUNT

Note: To do this activity, you should be using a word processing program.

This game has two challenges: First find each of the keys listed in column one on a computer keyboard. Then match up the key name with the descriptions in column two.

1. Start with column one. Find the key listed on your keyboard.

2. When you have found the key, find out what it does.

3. Then match the name of the key with the definition in the right-hand column.

Home	Moves cursor up a whole screen.
Shift	Moves cursor to the end of a word, line, or document.
Insert	Turns every character you type into a capital letter.
Page Up	Turns every character you type into a capital letter when you hold it down.
End	Lets you type new characters in between other characters.
Caps Lock	Moves cursor to the beginning of a word, line, or document.
Esc	Moves cursor down a whole screen.
Page Down	Lets you leave what you are doing.

If you can locate these keys and tell what they do in your word processing program, you can be an Editing Champ. But BEWARE: If anyone finds out, they will come to YOU for help with word processing!

GRAPHICS ARE GREAT!

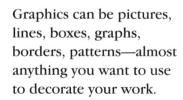

What Are Graphics?

Your computer can put two kinds of information on the screen. The **alphanumeric** kind is made up of letters and numbers. Just about anything else is called graphics.

Graphics can be pictures, lines, boxes, graphs, borders, patterns—almost anything you want to use to decorate your work.

Graphics programs are a special type of software, one which helps you draw more easily. The software will also help you change the pictures you have drawn with it.

There are many graphics programs such as Bannermania and Print Shop. You can use them to make greeting cards, calendars, and posters. You can make signs for your lemonade stand, flyers to advertise your lawn-mowing service, or paper banners for your baseball team. How about your own personal note paper, with your name and address, and a picture of something you really like? Or how about

your own magazine—complete with drawings?

Graphics programs come with their own pictures (**clip art**). You can use these pictures in your own designs. If you have a color printer, the clip art will even print in color.

BUZZ WORDS

al•pha•nu•mer•ic
clip art
graph•ics
paint and draw
pix•els

Paint and Draw Programs

S ome of the newer graphics programs will let you draw your own artwork and

looks like a group of little dots. These dots are called **pixels**.

Erase— This tool wipes out parts of your picture when you tell it to— without tearing or smearing, because it isn't on paper yet!

Line Draw—This tool will help you draw a straight line with your mouse—without a ruler.

A **Text**—Would you like to write something on your design? Text is the tool for typing words on the screen.

Square —This one will draw a perfect square or rectangle—every time you tell it to. It's great for drawing houses or buildings.

Circle —This one works just like the square tool, only it makes circles and egg shapes.

save it in your computer. Imagine—no mess, no paint to spill, and all the color you can use!

These graphics programs are called **paint and draw** programs, because that is what you do with them— in your computer. You use your mouse to draw a picture on the screen, and the graphics program gives you colors and patterns you can use to make your picture look just the way you want it to.

Paint and draw programs have other small programs in them called *tools*. Just

like real tools, they are there to help you make things. Here are some of the tools you will find in a paint and draw program:

Fill—This tool helps you color a picture without going outside the lines.

Spray —This tool works like a can of spray paint. It leaves a fine mist of color wherever you aim it.

Magnify—This tool is also called Zoom. It works like a magnifying glass, making a part of your picture so large that it

Super Graphic Projects You Can Do

1. Colorful banners for birthdays, holidays, special events, or school activities—big enough to hang across a wall.

2. One-of-a-kind holiday cards, birthday greetings, Get Well cards, or Thank-you notes.

3. Job flyers. Have you started a business— babysitting, lawn mowing, or walking dogs?

Spread the word!

4. Posters for lost-and-found items, school activities (dances, elections, sports events)—or your own pictures to put up in your room.

5. School assignments. Try making a cover page for a book report, or a chart for your science project.

6. Gifts. How about making some stationery as a gift for a friend? All you have to do is make up one page and print it out. Then take it to a copy shop. The copy shop can make copies and put them in a tablet.

7. Certificates. Are you a member of a team or group? You can make certificates for all the members. Just make one up and have it copied.

For Writers Only

If you want to do some fancy things with words and pictures, *graphic writing programs* will help you do it. You can create pictures of dinosaurs, aliens, houses, cars—and a story to go with the pictures. (Did you ever want to write your own comic strip? Try it with one of these programs!)

The World of Computer Games

You have a busy day ahead. After school, you are going to cruise the Amazon looking for a jewel thief. That shouldn't take more than an hour. Then you will have to do a quick change so you can take on the World Tae Kwan Do Champion. If you hurry, there might be time before dinner to help a poor spaceship janitor save the universe. What are you doing? Playing computer games!

Computer games are programs that do the "job" of playing a game. They tell the computer how to make the pictures and sounds of the game. Computer games can be about sports, adventures, or *fantasy* (make-believe and magic). You can play computer games by yourself, with a partner, or in teams.

Would you like to travel through an adventure that you helped to make up? Then role-playing games are for you. A role is a make-believe person you can pretend to be. In a *role-playing game*, the computer shows you what it looks like when you pretend.

Educational games are full of facts you can use in school. They can help you find fun in almost any subject. In one educational game, you can travel around the world— and through time— chasing a criminal named Carmen Sandiego. You will need to learn a lot about history and geography if you are going to catch her!

Do you like sports? There are *computer sports games* for football, baseball, hockey, and more! You have to use all your knowledge of the sport to beat your opponent.

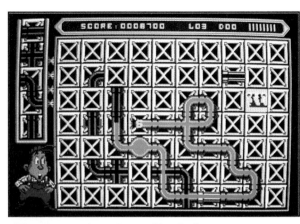

Pipe Dream, from Lucasfilm, Ltd.

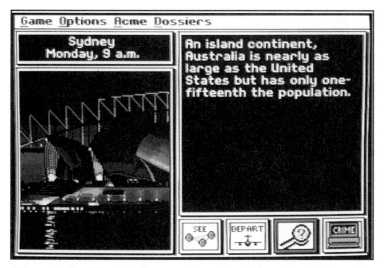

Where in the World is Carmen Sandiego?, from Broderbund.

Joysticks

A **joystick** is an input device that is shaped like a handle, or a pistol grip with no pistol attached. You may have used one at a video game arcade. There are joysticks that work the same way for personal computers. They help you to shoot when you play target games. They make it easy to steer when you play flying or driving games.

The arrow keys on your keyboard will let you steer, so you don't really need a joystick for computer games. They are just fun to use!

Did you ever wish you could fly a plane? In **simulation games**, you can pretend to do exciting things like flying a plane or a spaceship. You learn about all the controls, get a mission, and the rest is up to you! (Some flight simulation games look so real, pilots use them for practice.)

Play and Learn

A great thing about computer games is that while you play, you also learn. Practice makes your eyes and hands work together. You can practice your thinking skills as you learn to "outwit" the game. And of course, your computer skills keep getting better!

Spell It Plus, from Davidson & Associates.

Nintendo, Move Over—Here Come the Personal Computers!

The Nintendo Game System is a famous machine that is made only for playing games. It is a **dedicated** computer. (Dedicated means a computer is made to do just one thing, and nothing else.)

Dedicated computers used to be best for playing games. But personal computers are getting better. Here are some reasons why.

- If your computer has a special part called a **sound card**, your computer can sound as good as a stereo.

- If you have a color monitor, your computer games will be in color. Some of them look better than television pictures.

- You can store and save games on a personal computer. (You can't do that on a dedicated game computer.)

- In many computer games, you can type instructions for the people in the game to follow. This can make your games much more fun. (A dedicated game computer can't take any new instructions.)

- You can use a personal computer to run many different programs from graphics to math. A dedicated computer can run game programs.

Some new personal computers can run games just as well as dedicated game computers, and maybe even better. Explore what your computer can do!

Where Did Computer Games Come From?

Like computers themselves, computer games have a history. They have been around for longer than you might think!

1958 *Pong.* This was the first known computer game. It looked like a simple picture of ping pong. A dot bounced back and forth between two short lines that worked like paddles. A researcher at Brookhaven National Library made up the game. It was made to show off the Library's computers to visitors.

1962 *Space War.* This was the first space game. It was made up (and played first) at Harvard University. In the 1960s, people who used computers for work began to make up more space games for fun. But there were no personal computers yet.

1971 *Computer Space.* Integrated circuits were brand new. This complicated space game used them. It was one of the first arcade games. You could fly your spaceship with a joystick, jump to hyper-space, shoot at other ships, or orbit around a star—even change the star so it pushed you away or pulled you in! This game was too fancy for most people. Not very many played it.

BUZZ WORDS

ar•cade game

en•ter•tain•ment

port•a•ble

re•search•er

ver•sion

1973 *Pong.* This was another early arcade game. It was an improved version of the first *Pong*, and it used knobs to move the paddles.

Early 1970s *Odyssey* (early 1970s). This was Pong played on a home television screen. Video games were starting to catch on, but they were very simple, and they had to have their own input devices. There were still

Quick Click

The first computer games were played on mainframes. These computers were the size of a room, and they cost about 8 million dollars each!

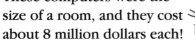

no personal computers yet.

 Death Race. This game started a controversy—people argued about whether it was good or bad. The arcade game had a steering wheel. The wheel steered a little video picture of a car. You had to drive through a place that looked like a graveyard, and hit moving creatures that were shaped like people. When you hit a creature, it turned into a gravestone, and then you would have to steer around the stone. The more creatures you hit, the higher your score was. In 1975, arcade games were still new, but thousands of people were playing them. Some of the players thought *Death Race* was fun. Other players thought it was wrong to make a game out of running over creatures who looked like people.

 Space Invaders. This arcade game was also a fight with creatures, but it took place on the moon—and the creatures were shooting back. Created in Japan, *Space Invaders* became an instant hit. Many more Japanese arcade games followed.

 Asteroids. This was another shoot-'em-up-in-space game. You had to blast the asteroids (big space rocks) and keep your ship away from them. In the early versions of the game, the asteroids were very simple graphics in black and white—but they moved around quickly.

 Pac Man. Pac Man was a full color arcade game. It combined a maze with a haunted house. Pac Man was a yellow ball with a mouth. He ate up a string of dots in the maze, while keeping away from colorful ghosts. This game was a super hit.

> T he idea for the *Death Race* game came from a movie called "Death Race 2000." It was about a future world where people used cars to kill other people as a sport.
>
> The National Traffic Safety Council teaches people to drive safely. The Council said the Death Race game was teaching people to drive badly, and teaching them not to care if they hurt other people. The makers of the game said the game was only fun and make-believe. What do you think?

Back to Computers in the 1980s.

The silicon chip came into use in the 1980s, and three things happened to computer games:

1. As computers got smaller, more people bought them and took them home. Games for personal computers started to catch on, because more people had something to play them on.

2. Computer toys started to appear in stores. The Atari and Coleco game systems—which you played through a TV set—were two early computer toys. Later, as chips got smaller, portable computer games came out. By 1988, they would fit in a wrist watch. Today many other toys use computer chips.

3. As personal computers got better, computer games got complicated again. But this time people were ready for them—maybe because it was more fun to play complicated games at home. Each year the games became more interesting to play, and more challenging to win.

Quick Click

Arcade games are dedicated computers.

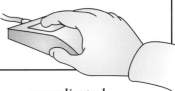

Today's home computers give the game programmers a chance to go all out. Some games have stereo music, and color graphics as sharp as a TV picture. What would the inventor of Pong think of them now?

Computer Games Today

Today, computers are an important form of entertainment—there are many ways to have fun with them. You can still find arcade games in shopping malls. You can play with dedicated game systems and other "smart" toys. Or you can try games that are as complicated as flight simulators, right on your personal computer.

GETTING ORGANIZED WITH
DATABASES

A database is a collection of data, or information.

You use databases all the time, but you might not even know it. If you looked at the sports page this morning to find the scores, you were looking at a kind of database. If you looked up a number in a phone book, you used another database. Dictionaries, cookbooks, and address books are databases. Any collection of information is a database if it is organized, and if it is **updated**. You update a database when you take out any outdated information and put in new, "up-to-date" information.

A database program is just a computer version of the same thing. But because computers work so fast, they can make the

information easy to find and update.

If you want to keep track of a lot of things or people—or ideas of your own—a database program can help you do it!

How It Works

Let's say you have used your computer to create a database of your baseball cards, how many you have, when you got them, how much you paid for each one, and what condition each one is

in. Your database will have places to put every fact about the players, such as name, team, and batting average. Then there will be information about the cards themselves.

Each fact is a piece of information called a **field**. All the information from one card is called a **record**. The program can sort this information rapidly.

Let's say you want to know what you paid for your Ken Griffey, Jr. cards

because you are getting ready to trade two of them to your friend. Instead of looking through each card and searching for notes on what you paid for them, you would just type in a command to the computer. Out comes a report telling you what you need to know. And all in less than a second!

Database Ideas

You could make a database of the videocassette movies your family has. That might make it easier for everyone to choose which ones to watch.

A database of your video games might be useful— you could tell which ones you have lent out, and who may have borrowed them. You could also keep track of your top score, and the top scores of your friends.

You might have a database of all the phone numbers of the kids in your class. That might make it easier

to send out birthday party invitations.

How are Databases Used?

Databases are used in lots of ways.

Schools may keep report cards or attendance records on the computer.

The library uses a database to see who has taken out what books and when.

Airlines use databases to keep track of who is flying, when, where, how much the tickets cost—and if any seats are available.

Where would YOU expect to find databases? (Think about who might need a LOT of information—fast!)

You Be the Database

This activity will help you understand what a database can do for you. Remember, a database manages information. It lets you ask the computer for just the facts you want. Then the computer goes to the database and searches through all the information there. Once the searching is done, the output will tell you what you want to know. This output is usually called a report.

This chart shows what a report might look like. Each name, address, and number is in a separate field. The computer goes through all the fields in the database, and then puts them in the order you have asked it for.

To see what a database does, you will be working like the CPU in the computer—creating output from the list. Just follow the instructions in Report 1, and do the same for the rest of the reports.

IN THIS ACTIVITY, YOU TAKE THE PLACE OF THE COMPUTER.

For each report, sort through the database to find the answers.

Report 1: How many boys are signed up for the Computer Club? _____8_____

Report 2: How many girls are signed up for the Computer Club? _____

Report 3: How many members are in the 5th grade? _____

Report 4: How many members are in the 6th grade? _____

Report 5: How many members are in the 7th grade? _____

Report 6: How many members live on Meridian Street? _____

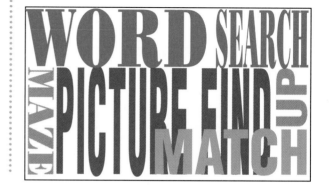

PARTICIPANTS IN THE COMPUTER CLUB

Name	Sex	Address	Telephone	Grade Level
Adams, Michael	M	4623 Everglade	555-3294	5
Brown, Greg	M	1234 Bonita	555-2908	6
DeCamp, Carol	F	Q5012 Park	555-5012	6
Ferris, Mark	M	909 E. 67th	555-7520	7
Graham, Amber	F	4670 Illinois	555-6921	5
Hill, Bob	M	5789 Meridian	555-2692	6
Jacobs, Tara	F	6544 College	555-7824	5
Kelly, Maureen	F	201 Waldron	555-9388	6
Monroe, John	M	1716 Thompson	555-7302	7
Newman, Nancy	F	5858 Crittenden	555-3402	6
Potter, Bill	M	7520 Illinois	555-3710	5
Resnick, Megan	F	4327 Everglade	555-9875	7
Turner, Joe	M	4678 College	555-8967	5
Vitz, Annie	F	5697 Meridian	555-7313	6
Woodson, Jack	M	7515 Holly	555-3456	5

MIX 'EM UP!

All these words are a little mixed up. With a little help from you, we can get these computer terms in correct order. Good luck!

RCEMPOTU _____

NTOF _____

DMOME _____

SLPIREHPREA _____

PHCI _____

DRASPETHESE _____

SRNTOISRAT _____

CRSGHPIA _____

PYOPFL KDSI _____

RNOTMOI _____

TRPIERN _____

DBROAYEK _____

SPREADSHEETS

Does it seem like money just disappears from your pockets?

Do you feel like you never know just where you spent your allowance? Does it seem like you can never save enough money to buy that special pair of shoes or new CD?

Maybe you need a **budget**. A budget is a way to help you show how much money you have, how you plan to save it or spend it, and how much you may have left over.

Many people and businesses use **spreadsheet** programs. A spreadsheet can help you keep track of the money you have, the money you

BUZZ WORDS

budg•et

cell

spread•sheet

spend, and the money you have left. Once you know all that, you've set up a **budget**.

How It Works

A spreadsheet sets up rows and columns of information. For a budget, each *row* descibes a different thing you might spend your money on—books, gifts, candy, etc.

The spreadsheet also has *columns* that go up and down the screen. These columns are for measuring time. They can tell you where your money goes

REGGIE'S
BANK-N-BUDGET
STORE

MY MONTHLY BUDGET

	A	B	C	D	E	F
1	January	February		April	May	J...
2						
3	Savings	$10.00	9.6	6.00	$ 3	.65
4	Books	$ 7.35	2.8	$1 .00	$ 3.	95
5			2.50	$		
				$ 7.25		
				$16.50	$ 9.4	

from day to day, week to week, month to month or year to year.

Each box that is formed by rows and columns is called a **cell**. You write names and numbers in the cells, and when the computer calculates a math problem, it puts the answer in a cell.

Why Use a Spreadsheet?

You could do this on paper, but a computer spreadsheet makes it easier. Let's say you are keeping track of your allowance or your savings. If the amount is changed, you can tell the program what the new amount is. The program will change the amounts in the cells for you. Then it will tell you how much money you have left over.

Now all you need is a program to tell you how to get a bigger allowance!

CAI

IT'S SPECIAL SOFTWARE YOU SHOULD KNOW ABOUT

The computer can be used as a great learning tool. Computer programs that are made just for learning are called **Computer-Aided Instruction** programs. This type of software is called **CAI** for short.

Improve Your skills

There are hundreds of programs that have been written to help kids and students learn. They are on almost any subject.

One of these types of programs is called a **drill and practice**. You may have used drill and practice programs in math class, to practice multiplication, addition, and subtraction. These programs are like using flash cards to practice your skills, but they are a lot more fun.

Improve Your Imagination

Another kind of CAI program is a **simulation**.

A simulation makes pretending more like real life. A simulation program might take you on a pretend trip to the moon in a rocket, or across the West in a covered wagon. It shows you pictures, gives you facts and asks you questions as if the trip were really happening. You get to choose the things you will take along and the way you will go, and make sure that you

don't run out of food—then you get to watch the simulation and see if you made good choices! Simulations can help you see how people use the things they know. This might help you with science, history, and other subjects.

When you are ready to finish high school, there are CAI programs that tell you all about different jobs and colleges, and help you decide which is best for you. In the meantime, if you need help at school, ask your teacher if your school has CAI programs you can use.

Oregon Trail, from MECC.

MIX 'EM UP!

All these words are also a little mixed up! With a little help from you, we can get these computer terms in correct order. Good luck!

TUROCULACL ——————————

TROLHELHI ————————————

EGNARTIDET TRUICCI ————————

QUJDRACA ——————————————

SOROSREPC ———————————————

IRACTIHEMT CLOGI NTUI ——————

ROUPTNIT——————————

ELRAS ————————————

YANIBR ————————————

GOPTICRYH ————————

SLEIXP————————————

TASMUINILSO —————————

HIDDEN COMPUTERS

Computers are all around us— and not just on our desks!

Many of today's machines have dedicated computers inside them. As you know, dedicated computers are programmed to do one job. You cannot program them for any purpose other than the job they were made for.

There are 12 things with dedicated computers hidden in this picture. How many can you find?

Hint: One of the hidden computers is a remote control for a television.

THE BIGGEST
HIDDEN COMPUTER?

HOME   VISITORS

...DO THE WAVE...

We've all seen them in every professional football and basketball arena—giant television scoreboards. Remember? The boards usually declare the last play as...

...AWESOME...AWESOME...AWESOME!

The scoreboard does more than display the score and time left in the game. Sometimes it shows an athlete's face or replays a big catch. Sometimes the scoreboard encourages the crowd to do the WAVE. Don't you wonder who is running that computer? Because that's what it is—a dedicated computer, with the scoreboard for an output device!

CROSSWORD CHALLENGE

Test your computer knowledge!

ACROSS

2. Name given to a collection of computer data that is stored.

4. Category of computer program used to create a budget.

5. Category of computer program used when you have lots of information to keep track of.

6. _____ matrix printer.

7. Output device that has a screen.

8. Output device that prints on paper.

DOWN

1. Sometimes called a floppy, it stores computer data.

3. Input device that you type at.

5. Holds the diskette in the CPU

HIDDEN DATABASES

With all the hidden computers around, there surely must be hidden databases, too. Think about it. Any time you use a credit card, or see your grades on a computer form, or see the pizza parlor entering your family's name into their computer, don't you wonder why that information is being saved?

The database may be used to help that place serve it's customers better. It might be serving other purposes too.

Sometimes the database your family's name is on is sold to other companies. This can be a good thing, if the company is selling something you need. But often they just want to send you "junk mail."

Some countries use big databases to keep track of their citizens. This can help them decide how to run the country, and control crime.

Let's look at some of the things they might know— right here in the United States:

Facts about you when you were born. When a child is born, the hospital computer records the parents' names, the place, the date, and the time, and medical information about the baby.

Your Social Security number.

Where you go to school. Your name and Social Security number are entered into a database at school. Then they are sent to another database in your state capital.

These are only a few of the facts the government knows.

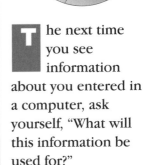

The next time you see information about you entered in a computer, ask yourself, "What will this information be used for?"

Luckily, there are strict laws about how this information can be used. Your family has a right to keep important information private. But there are also people (such as doctors) who might really need that information in case they need to help you.

People have different feelings about what should be done with the information in big databases. What do you think?

CAREERS IN COMPUTERS

It used to be that anybody who worked with computers had to be a genius. They had job titles like:

Nuclear Physicist
Analytical Engineer
Systems Programmer
Computer Technician

Today people who work with computers can be called:

Writer
Cashier
Sales Clerk
Reservationist
Doctor
Mechanic
Athlete

When you choose a career, you will have more choices if you are comfortable around computers. Almost every job today can use a computer in some way.

Here are a few ways that computers are used in jobs. Is there one you would like to work in?

Computers in the News

The next time you watch the news on TV, watch what happens as the show begins. Letters appear from nowhere, and go together to make words on the TV screen. Sometimes there are moving patterns behind the words. Sometimes a world globe seems to float in midair.

When the newscaster begins a story a picture or a film may seem to appear on the wall behind the newscaster. The pictures and films are not really showing on the wall. How is it done? These interesting sights are called *special effects*, and many of them are made using a computer. Someone has the job of using a computer to turn the pictures into part of

REGGIE'S NATIONAL BANK

the signal that goes out to your television set.

Most of these fancy effects are set up before the show begins. The computers are programmed to show the pictures and films at just the right time. They can even make the clouds swirl on the weather map.

These days, television stations could almost be called computer stations!

Computers In Baseball

Many baseball teams now use computers to improve their game!

Some teams use the Baseball Information System. This is a database made by IBM. It has information about many players—how well they play, how much money they make, and when their teams are playing. Some teams use databases to

keep track of how each player performs in every game.

Computers in Medicine

C omputers are everywhere in medicine. When you go to get your eyes checked, a computer takes pictures of your eyes. Other computers take measurements of your eyes, and help to make the lenses for your glasses.

In the hospital, computers are just as busy. They help give medicine to patients. They keep track of people who are very sick or badly hurt. They help the doctors and nurses decide what to do.

Some people have tiny dedicated computers planted inside their bodies to help them.

A doctor might put one called a pacemaker inside a person's heart to make it work better.

Doctors are finding more ways to use computers all the time. If you become a doctor or nurse someday, you will also be working with computers.

CROSSWORD CHALLENGE

Test your computer mastery!

ACROSS

2. Beginner's All-purpose Symbolic Instructional Code.

4. Main ingredient in a computer chip.

5. Computer-Aided Instruction.

6. A program that makes pretending more like real life.

7. The blinking light on a computer screen that tells where the next keystroke will go.

8. Englishman who designed the Analytical Engine with help from the Countess of Lovelace.

10. Random-Access Memory.

14. Computer typeface.

15. _____ processing.

DOWN

1. Path that electricity follows inside the computer.

2. To move your cursor back one keystroke.

3. Central Processing Unit.

6. Ready-made programs.

8. Binary Digit.

9. Read-Only Memory.

11. Name of the key used to type a capital letter instead of a lowercase letter.

12. Computer language used by the military, it was named for the Countess of Lovelace.

13. Sets of instructions that tell a computer what to do.

WHO'S WHO IN COMPUTERS
HOLLYWOOD STYLE!

Computers have been in movies for a long time. In the 1957 movie *Desk Set*, a mainframe almost takes over a TV station! In a movie made in 1970, a mainframe named *Colossus* takes over the world. Most of the movie *Tron* (1982) takes place *inside* a computer!

There have been many famous computers and robots in movies and TV shows. See if you can match the computer or robot on this list with the movie or TV shows they appeared in.

The robots and computers:

Commander Data

HAL-9000

Cylons

R2D2

KITT

Robby the Robot

C3PO

JOSHUA

SAL-9000

VINCENT

Rosie

Number 5

VALCOM 17485

Dot Matrix

WORD SEARCH
MAZE PICTURE FIND UP MATCH

The shows:

Heartbeeps

The Empire Strikes Back

Forbidden Planet

Spaceballs

Star Trek: The Next Generation

Wargames

The Black Hole

Battlestar Galactica

Short Circuit

Star Wars

The Jetsons

2001: A Space Odyssey

Knight Rider

2010: The Year We Make Contact

CAN COMPUTERS TAKE OVER THE WORLD?

Well, they have. Lots of times. But only on TV and in movies!

In real life, even the most powerful computer can only follow instructions. Even though it works fast, people have to tell it what to do. Here's an example.

Let's say you're using a computer to keep track of your baseball cards, and you ask it for a printout of ALL the stats on EVERY player who played for the Chicago Cubs from 1985 to 1992. The machine can sort through thousands of facts—almost instantly—and decide which of the players belong on the printout. But it can only do this because a person has given it instructions on how to do every single step in the process. Computer "monsters" are fun to imagine, but not real.

COMPUTERS AND THE FUTURE

Computers have come a long way since the days of UNIVAC. But that was only about 40 years ago (a short time when you compare it to all of history).

If we tried to use UNIVAC, we might laugh because it seems so big and clumsy. But the people who built UNIVAC could not know what computers would be like today. If you could go back in time and tell them about personal computers, THEY would laugh at such a "crazy" idea. To them, it would mean that everybody in the 1990s must be a millionaire!

Computers have changed so much, it is hard to believe they will go on changing. But people will keep finding new things to do with them. There will be new hardware and new software. Maybe someday you will have a tiny computer that fits in a pencil—or a pocket terminal that can talk to a giant mainframe, and tell you anything you want to know. What changes do you think would make computers better? Someone may be working on that improvement right now!

Write a story or draw a picture about a time traveler from the year 2099 who comes to visit your class. She laughs because she thinks personal computers are too big and clumsy. She tells you about the computers they have in 2099. How big are they? Where are they used? What are they used for? What happens when they break down? What new things can the software do? How are they different from today's computers? Are they better or worse?

THINK ABOUT IT

GLOSSARY

abacus (AB-a-kuss): ancient Chinese device for adding and subtracting numbers.

alphanumeric (AL-fa-noo-MAIR-ick): letters and numbers.

arcade game (ar-KADE game): a *dedicated* computer that runs a coin-operated game.

Arithmetic Logic Unit (air-ith-MET-ick LOJ-ick YOO-nit): the part of the *processor* that handles the calculation of numbers.

ASCII (ASK-ee): American Standard Code for Information Interchange, a common *binary code*.

Babbage, Charles (BAB-age): an English mathematician and inventor who lived from 1792 to 1871. He helped found the Royal Astronomical Society, and (with Lady Ada *Lovelace*) designed a mechanical computer called the **Analytical Engine** (an-a-LIT-ih-kal EN-jin).

binary code (BY-nair-ee code): *data* written as 1's and 0's, which represent electric pulses.

bit (bit): the smallest piece of *data* a computer can use.

budget (BUDJ-et): a plan for saving and spending money.

BBS: abbreviation for Bulletin Board System (BUL-le-tin board SIS-tem), and another name for **electronic bulletin board** (ee-lek-TRON-ick BUL-le-tin board). This feature of an *online service* lets customers trade information by *modem*.

byte (bite): eight *bits* of *data. Memory* is measured in **kilobytes** (KIL-o-bytes) or thousands of bits, and in **megabytes** (MEG-uh-bytes) or millions of bits.

calculator (KAL-kyu-late-or): a machine for doing math problems.

category (KAT-uh-gor-ee): a collection of things that all have the same important feature in common.

central processing unit (SEN-tral PROS-ess-ing YU-nit): the computer's "brain," which carries out commands for working with data. Abbreviated CPU.

cells: the places in the *display* shown by a *spreadsheet* where you put numbers in.

character (KARE-ak-ter): a letter, number, punctuation mark, or symbol. Characters Per Second (abbreviated **CPS**) means how fast a *printer* can write.

chip (chip): a single *integrated circuit* in the *CPU*.

circuit((SIR-kit): a path that electricity follows.

clip art: *graphic* images that are part of graphics *software*.

compatible (kom-PAT-ih-bul): able to use *programs* that were made to be run on another type of computer. Most *systems* made by *IBM* and Apple Computer before 1992 were not compatible with each other.

component (kom-POH-nent): a part of a machine that is needed in order for it to work, or a machine that is part of a *system*. *Peripherals* such as the *monitor* are components.

computer (kom-PUTE-er): a machine that computes (works with *data* in the form of numbers).

Computer-Aided Instruction (kom-PUTE-er AID-ed in-STRUK-shun): using computers — especially with *educational* programs such as *simulations* or *drill and practice* — to help with school work and tests. Abbreviated **CAI**.

computer language (kom-PUTE-er LANG-wij): one of many special languages used for telling the computer what to do. Two types are *high-level language* and *programming language*.

continuous-feed (kon-TIN-yu-us FEED): computer paper that feeds automatically through a *printer* as one long sheet.

Control Unit (kon-TROL YOO-nit): the part of the *processor* that moves your information from one step to the next.

copyrighted (KOP-ee-rite-ed): not to be copied without permission from the maker. Most books, records, and *software* products are protected by copyright laws.

cursor (KUR-sor): a dot of light on the *monitor* screen that tells you where the next *character* will go.

data (DAY-tuh): building blocks for information. Facts are data. Information is an organized set of facts.

database (DAY-tuh-base): a collection of organized *data*. Database *programs* put data into a database and get it out.

dedicated (DED-ih-cate-ed): a computer that is built to do only one job. Bank teller machines are dedicated computers.

digital (DIJ-ih-tal): turned into numbers (digits). You can use a computer to create information from digital *data*.

disk drive (DISK drive): a computer's place for *magnetic disks*. It is a slot for *floppy disks*, or a sealed *hard disk* unit.

display (dih-SPLAY): the information shown by a computer on the *monitor* screen.

document (DOK-yu-ment): an organized body of information that is small enough to work on. Anything you write using your *word processor* is a document. When a *database* searches for information and shows it to you, that information is also a document.

dot-matrix printer (dot MAY-trix PRINT-er): a type of *printer* that uses pins to make ink dots that form letters.

drill and practice (drill and PRAK-tiss): a type of *software* used for *Computer-Aided Instruction*.

edit (ED-it): to change written work you have already done.

electronic (ee-lek-TRON-ick): a type of device that works by shooting electric particles called electrons through a *vacuum tube*, *transistor*, or *integrated circuit*.

ENIAC (EE-nee-ak): name of a successful *mainframe* built during World War II. Its name stands for *Electronic* Numerical Integrator And *Calculator*.

field: a place on the screen to put *data* into a *database*. All the fields in one database *file* are a **record**.

file (file): the place on a *magnetic disk* where you *store* the *data* you have been working with.

floppy disk (FLOP-py disk): a removable *magnetic disk* which holds less information than a *hard disk*. It fits into its own *disk drive*, and is used to load *software* and *data* into the computer. Also called a **diskette**.

font (fahn't): a complete set of letters and numbers that look like they belong together (also called a **typeface**).

graphic (GRAF-ick): made up of pictures.

hard disk (hard disk): a *magnetic disk* with a large amount of *memory*, sealed in its own container and built into the computer.

hardware (HARD-ware): the devices that make up a computer *system*.

high-level language (hi LEV-el LANG-wij): High-level computer languages are used for creating *software* and other *programs*. *ADA* is a high-level language.

Hollerith, Herman (HOL-ler-ith): the American inventor of the **Tabulating Machine** (TAB-yu-late-ing ma-SHEEN), and founder of *IBM*. He lived from 1860 to 1929.

IBM (eye-bee-EM): abbreviation for International Business Machines (IN-ter-NA-shun-al BIZ-ness ma-sheens), the first maker of *mainframe* computers.

input (IN-put): *data* going into a computer.

install (in-STAHL): to put a *program* on the computer's *hard disk*, or tell the program what kind of computer it's running on.

integrated circuit (IN-tih-grate-ed SIR-kit): a 1958 invention that put all the circuits a computer needs in one place. The integrated circuit is the basis of the computer *chip*.

Jacquard, Joseph-Marie (shak-KAR): a French weaver and inventor who lived from 1752 to 1834.

Jacquard Loom (shak-KAR loom): an automatic loom invented in 1801 by Joseph-Marie *Jacquard*. It used instructions from punched cards to weave cloth.

joystick (JOY-stick): an *input* device often used for *simulation games*. Joysticks can be shaped like an airplane's control stick, a pistol grip without a pistol, or a handle on a pivot.

keyboard (KEY-board): a *peripheral* that looks like a typewriter with extra keys. You use a keyboard to type *input* into the computer.

laser printer (LAZE-er PRINT-er): a *printer* that uses *data* from the *computer* and a laser create *characters* with toner.

Leibnitz, Gottfried (LIBE-nitz): a German mathematician and inventor who lived from 1646 to 1716. He invented a hand-held mechanical *calculator*.

Lovelace, Lady Ada Augusta Byron, Countess of Lovelace (LOVE-lace): the English mathematician who invented *programs*. She lived from 1815 to 1852, and was the daughter of a famous poet. The high-level *computer language* ADA (used to create aerospace and military *programs*) is named after her.

Macintosh (MACK-in-tosh): a brand of *personal computer* introduced in 1984 by Apple Computer, Inc.

magnetic disk (mag-NET-ick disk): a disk that stores information as a pattern of magnetic particles on its surface. There are two types: *floppy disks* and *hard disks*.

mainframe (MAIN-frame): the largest and earliest type of *electronic* computer. Modern mainframes can handle huge numbers, and many people can use them at once.

Mark I: *mainframe* built to help with calculations for the atomic bomb project in World War II.

memory (MEM-o-ree): the part of the *processor* where the computer stores *data*. There are two types: *RAM* and *ROM*.

microcomputer (MY-kro-kom-PUTE-er): a *personal computer*, which is very small ("micro") compared to a *mainframe*.

minicomputer (MIN-ee-kom-PUTE-er): a small ("mini") *mainframe* which has *terminals* so several people can use it at once.

modem (MOH-dem): a device that connects a computer to a telephone line. Its name stands for MOdulator/ DEModulator. The **answer modem** is on the receiving end of a telephone call. The **originate modem** (oh-RIJ-ih-nate MOH-dem) makes the call.

monitor (MON-ih-tor): a TV-like device for displaying *output*.

mouse (mouse): a hand-sized *input* device that moves a pointer on the *monitor* screen.

online service (on-line SER-viss): a service for computer users that can have features such as a *BBS* and a *database*.

operating system (OP-er-ate-ing SIS-tem): a *program* that tells the computer how to run other programs.

output (OUT-put): information coming out of a computer.

paint and draw (paint and draw): a type of program that lets you make *graphic* images on your computer screen.

Pascal, Blaise, (pas-KAL): a French scientist, mathematician, and inventor who lived from 1623-1662.

Pascaline (pas-ka-LEEN): an adding machine invented by Blaise *Pascal*.

path (path): the route your *data* follows through the computer.

peripheral (puh-RIF-er-ul): a device that is connected to a computer to give it *input* or to take its *output*.

personal computer (PER-sa-nul kom-PUTE-er): another name for a *microcomputer* made to be used by just one person.

pixels (PICKS-ells): dots that make up an image on a screen.

platen (PLATE-en): the roller for paper in a *printer*.

portable (PORT-a-bul): easy to carry around. Some *personal computers* are portable.

printer (PRINT-er): a *peripheral* that prints *output* on paper. Two types are *dot-matrix* and *laser printers*.

processor (PROSS-ess-or): the part of the *CPU* that handles the flow of *data*.

program (PROH-gram): a set of instructions, written in *computer language*, that tells the computer what to do and how to do it. Programmers are the people who write these instructions, and programming is the name for what they do.

programming language (PROH-gram-ing LANG-wij): a *computer language* that changes words and numbers into electric pulses (so the computer can respond to our commands), and changes the electric pulses back into words and numbers (so we can understand what the computer has done).

publisher (PUB-lish-er): a company that makes *software* to sell.

public domain (PUB-lick doh-MAIN): free to be used by anyone.

RAM (ram): abbreviation for **Random-Access Memory** (RAN-dom AK-sess MEM-o-ree): the part of the *memory* that is erased when you shut the computer off. It holds the *program* the computer is using.

ROM (rahm): abbreviation for **Read-Only Memory** (read ON-ly MEM-o-ree), the part of the *memory* that is not erased when you turn the computer off. It gets the computer ready to use *programs*.

save: to *store data* in a *file* or in *memory.*.

sequence (SEE-kwenss): events happening one after another. Computers see *data* as a sequence of electric pulses.

software (SOFT-ware): ready-made *programs* for the computer. Software is what runs on the *hardware*. Software that has had the newest features of its *program* put in by the *publisher* is called a *version* (VER-zhun).

silicon (SIL-ih-kon): a mineral that is found in sand. Computer *chips* are made of silicon.

simulation (sim-yu-LAY-shun): using a computer to practice or show activities that are similar to real activities.

spreadsheet (SPRED-sheet): a program that works like an automatic *calculator* for keeping track of money and making *budgets*.

store (store): to put information in a *file* on a *magnetic disk*, or in a computer's *memory*, so it can be used later.

system (SIS-tem): several devices that are connected, or made to work together. A computer and its *peripherals* are one type of system. Several connected computers that are used for *networking* are another type of system.

terminal (TUR-mih-nul): a combination *keyboard* and *monitor* that is connected to a *mainframe* or *minicomputer*.

thesaurus (the-SAUR-us): the part of a *word processor* that helps you find synonyms.

toner (TONE-er): a black powder that turns into ink when a *laser printer* heats it.

transistor (tran-ZISS-tor): an electrical device invented in 1948. It replaced *vacuum tubes*, making computers smaller.

update: to replace old *data*.

UNIVAC (YU-nih-vak): the first successful *mainframe* made to be sold as a product. It was built by the Sperry-UNIVAC company. Its name stands for UNIVersal Automatic Computer.

vacuum tube (VAK-yoo-um tube): a *component* of early *electronic* devices like radios, TVs, and computers. Its wires were mounted in a glass tube with no air inside.

word processor (WORD PROSS-ess-or): a *program* for writing documents on the computer screen.

ANSWER SECTION!

This section is where you will find the answers to the puzzles and quizzes! There are also some hints and questions to help you find out more about computers.

You won't find "Think About It" answers here, because the answers you think up are ALL YOURS. Compare them with your friends' "Think About It" answers!

Sort It All Out: Early History (page 4)

Leibnitz Calculator—Gottfried Leibnitz

abacus—people in China

Analytical Engine—Charles Babbage and Lady Lovelace

Jacquard Loom—Joseph Marie Jacquard

Pascaline—Blaise Pascal

HINT: Did you notice how inventors' names often become part of their inventions' names?

Practice with Your Abacus (page 7):

35 + 7 = 42
47 + 65 = 112

HINT: If you're having trouble, remember that the beads in the smaller section of the abacus are worth 5 each. On the string for the 1s, one of these beads is worth 5. On the string for the 10s, one of these beads is worth 50. Try it again using the "worth 5" beads!

Figure It Out: How much did Herman earn? (page 10)

Herman's machine counted 62,622,250 people in the U.S. population. He charged the government 63 cents per 1,000 people he counted. First, find out how many times 1,000 will go into Herman's total:

62,622,250 / 1,000 = 62,622.25

Multiply this answer by 63 cents to get your final answer:

62,622.25 x $.63 = $39,452.02

In 1890, that was quite a lot of money.

What Happened When? (page 13)

The Leibnitz Calculator was invented in the middle 1600s.

The silicon chip was invented in 1968.

Jacquard invented the automatic loom in 1801.

The abacus was invented about 4000 years ago.

The transistor was invented in 1948.

Charles Babbage and Lady Lovelace worked on the Analytical Engine in 1839.

Pascal invented the Pascaline in 1641.

Herman Hollerith's Tabulating Machine was used in the United States Census in 1890.

The integrated circuit was invented in 1958.

QUESTION: New inventions often start by trying to make old inventions work better. Which inventions in the quiz did this?

Word Search (page 17)

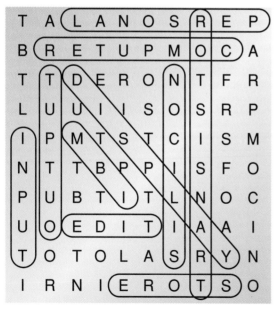

Find the Computer Parts! (page 20)

The central processing unit is hidden in shelf above the refrigerator.

The monitor is hidden in the oven door.

The keyboard is hidden in the refrigerator.

The mouse is hidden in the fruit bowl.

The printer is hidden on the stovetop.

QUESTION: Have you noticed how some machines look like other machines, but do very different jobs?

Word Search Number 2 (page 22)

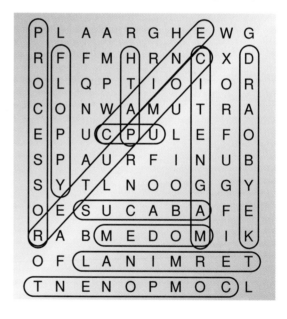

Mission Possible (page 30)

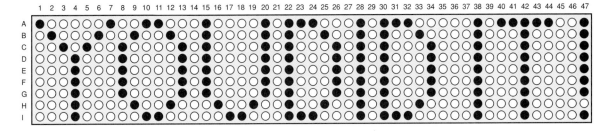

Fonts: Break the Code (page 33)

The message reads:

THIS IS A PERFECT FONT FOR SENDING MESSAGES TO MY BEST FRIEND.

QUESTIONS: Hieroglyphics (hy-ro-GLIFF-icks) are a kind of writing made up of pictures. The people of Egypt don't use hieroglyphics anymore. Why do you think they changed their writing? Are there other languages that use pictures in their writing? You may want to ask your English teacher about this.

A-MAZE-ING POWERS! (page 36)

Writing a Computer Program (page 38)

We forgot to tell the robot to put the lid back on the garbage can. We'd better rewrite that program before something starts to stink!

Break the Code! (page 42)

The message reads:

CONGRATULATIONS

The Great Keyboard Special Key Hunt (page 50)

Home takes you to the beginning of a word, line, or document.

Shift makes lowercase letters into capital letters.

Insert lets you put a new word in between other words.

Page Up moves the cursor up the screen.

End takes you to the end of a word, line, or document.

Caps Lock makes every letter you type a capital letter.

Esc lets you leave what you are doing.

Page Down moves the cursor down the page.

QUESTIONS: Do you know which of these keys can be found on a typewriter? Do you know which key the Enter key used to be?

You Be the Database (page 62)

Report 2: There are 7 girls signed up for the Computer Club.

Report 3: There are 6 members who are in the 5th grade.

Report 4: There are 6 members who are in the 6th grade.

Report 5: There are 3 members who are in the 7th grade.

Report 6: There are 2 members who live on Meridian Street.

QUESTION: How long did it take you to find the data? It would take a computer less than a second to find the data for each report.

Mix 'Em Up (page 63)

NTOF = *FONT*

DRASPETHESE = *SPREADSHEET*

DMOME = *MODEM*

SLPIREHPREA = *PERIPHERALS*

PHCI = *CHIP*

SRNTOISRAT = *TRANSISTOR*

CRSGHPIA = *GRAPHICS*

PYOPFL KDSI = *FLOPPY DISK*

RNOTMOI = *MONITOR*

TRPIERN = *PRINTER*

DBROAYEK = *KEYBOARD*

More Mix 'Em Up (page 67)

TUROCULACL = *CALCULATION*

TROLHELHI = *HOLLERITH*

EGNARTIDET TRUICCI = *INTEGRATED CIRCUIT*

QUJDRACA = *JACQUARD*

SOROSREPC = *PROCESSOR*

IRACTIHEMT CLOGI NTUI = *ARITHMETIC LOGIC UNIT*

ROUPTNIT = *PRINTOUT*

ELRAS = *LASER*

YANIBR = *BINARY*

GOPTICRYH = *COPYRIGHT*

SLEIXP = *PIXELS*

TASMUINILSO = *SIMULATION*

Hidden Computers (page 68)

Dedicated computers are hidden inside of:

digital watches

electrical thermometer (pictured)

toy car with remote control

digital scale

electric keyboard

microwave oven (pictured)

price gun

electric drum set (pictured)

television with remote

security camera

telephone

cash register

Crossword Challenge (page 70)

Across: 2.   FILE
             4.   SPREADSHEET
             5.   DATABASE

6. DOT
7. MONITOR
8. PRINTER

Down: 1. DISKETTE
3. KEYBOARD
5. DISKDRIVE

Crossword Challenge (page 74)

Across: 2. BASIC
4. SILICON
5. CAI
6. SIMULATION
7. CURSOR
8. BABBAGE
10. RAM
14. FONT
15. WORD

Down: 1. CIRCUIT
2. BACKSPACE
3. CPU
6. SOFTWARE
8. BIT
9. ROM
11. SHIFT
12. ADA
13. PROGRAM

Who's Who in Computers— Hollywood Style (page 75)

Commander Data is the robot crew member in *Star Trek: The Next Generation* (TV).

HAL-9000 is the mainframe aboard the spaceship in *2001: A Space Odyssey* (movie).

Cylons are enemy robots from space in *Battlestar Galactica* (TV series and movie).

R2D2 is the small robot in *Star Wars* (movie). (R2D2 and C3PO appear in all three Star Wars movies.)

SAL-9000 is the intelligent computer who stays on earth in *2010: The Year We Make Contact* (movie).

KITT is the car with a computer for a brain in *Knight Rider* (TV).

Robby the Robot helps the space travelers in *Forbidden Planet* (movie).

C3PO is the tall gold robot in *The Empire Strikes Back* (movie). (C3PO and R2D2 appear in all three Star Wars movies.)

JOSHUA is the mainframe in charge of nuclear weapons in *Wargames* (movie).

VINCENT is a brave robot in the space crew in *The Black Hole* (movie).

Rosie is the robot who cleans house in *The Jetsons* (TV series and movie).

Number 5 is the Army's robot weapon who becomes friendly in *Short Circuit* (movie).

VALCOM 17485 is a servant robot in *Heartbeeps* (movie).

Dot Matrix is the female robot who helps the princess in *Spaceballs* (movie).

QUESTIONS: Here are some questions to think about and talk about.

How many of these shows tell stories about space travel? How does NASA use computers?

How many of the shows tell stories about war? How do the armed forces use computers?

How many of the shows have robots that act like servants? Why would people have robot servants?

How many of the robots and computers have girls' names? What is the difference between a robot and a computer?

About the Authors

Cindra Tison and Mary Jo Woodside work with children, teachers, parents, and school administrators to improve their understanding and enjoyment of computers. They live in Indianapolis, Indiana.